New Creation Millennialism

New Creation Millennialism

J. Webb Mealy

Library of Congress Control Number: 2019910568

ISBN: 9781082468544

Contents

Preface 9

Chapter 1 Exposition of Rev. 19:5–21:8 11

Rev. 19:5–21:8—Narrative Context, or the Story So Far 11

Rev. 19:5–21:8 Brief Remarks on Composition and Structure 14

Exposition of Rev. 19:5-21 15

Introductory Remarks on Rev. 19:5-21 15

Exposition of Rev. 20:1-10 25

Summary Remarks on Rev. 20:1-10 37

Exposition of Rev. 20:11-15 38

Two Complications That Open Out to Further Theological Insights 44

Summary Remarks on Rev. 20:7-15 49

A Millennial Reign in Heaven above a Lifeless Earth? 50

Exposition of Rev. 21:1-8 51

Summary Remarks on Rev. 21:1-8 61

Chapter 2 Insurmountable Problems of Historic Premillennialism 63

Who Survives the Transition to the Age to Come? 65

When Does the New Creation Take Place? 74

When Does the New Jerusalem Come to Earth? 77

When Does the Wedding between Jesus and the New Jerusalem, His Bride, Take Place? 82

The Wedding of Jesus Christ, the Warrior King 82

Revelation 20: Two Interlocking Pairs of Visions 83

Revelation 21:1-8: Its Function Within the Vision Narrative 84

Jesus, Paul, and Peter on the Renewal of the Creation 89

Concluding Remarks: Implications—and Non-Implications—of These Findings 91

Chapter 3 Insurmountable Problems with Amillennialism 92

First Problem: When Resurrection Does Not Equal Resurrection 93

Second Problem: The Imprisonment and Release of Satan—A Fatal Dilemma 96

First Horn: The Battle of Rev. 20:7-10 is a Vision of the Beast's Career in Attacking the Church 97

Second Horn: The Battle of Rev. 20:7-10 is Not a Vision of the Beast's Career as a Whole, But Only of the Battle of Harmagedon 97

Third Problem: Expulsion from Heaven to Earth, or Capture and Imprisonment in the Abyss? 100

Chapter 4 Selective Resurrection in the New Testament: Rebutting the Main Amillennial Critique of Premillennialism 107

Jesus on "The Resurrection from among the Dead" 107

Paul on the Resurrection Hope of Believers 112

Christ's Kingdom—Here Now, or Not? 121

Christ's Coming Kingdom: Does it Last for One Age, or Does it Last Forever? 128

Chapters 1–4: Summary of Results 132

Conclusion 134

The Results of This Study 134

Concluding Theological Remarks 136

Appendix 1 Narrative Sections and Temporal Analysis That Underlie Chart 1 139

Appendix 2 Detailed Synopsis of Revelation and Isaiah 24–27 141

Appendix 3 A Brief Introduction to Previous Proponents of New Creation Millennialism 149

Early Church (70–300 CE) 149

Papias of Hierapolis (fl. c. 105–130 CE) 149

Epistle of Barnabas (c. 70–130 CE) 151

Melito, Bishop of Sardis (fl. c. 150–200 CE) 153

The Apocalypse of Elijah (c. 150–250 CE) 155

Methodius of Olympus (d. 311 CE) 156

Victorinus, Bishop of Pettau (d. c. 304 CE) 158

The Modern Period 161

John Gill 161

Sylvester Bliss 162

Wolfgang Metzger 163

Eckhard Schnabel 164

Summary 164

Index of References 165

Preface

Whereas amillennialism and postmillennialism have historically had great difficulty providing a coherent and plausible account of the internal literary workings of Rev. 19:11–20:10, historic premillennialism has faced every bit as much difficulty explaining how its "mixed age" reading of Rev. 20:1-10 can be reconciled with the promises to believers elsewhere in Revelation and with other eschatological expectations expressed both in Revelation and throughout the New Testament.

An interpretive option that is only rarely seen nowadays is to stay with a premillennial interpretive approach but understand that the millennium has the new creation as its setting. This approach neutralizes the most troublesome difficulties of premillennialism but raises a whole new crop of questions and interpretive challenges.

This essay will begin in Chapter 1 with an exposition of Rev. 19:5–21:8, which will demonstrate the naturalness and interpretive power of the view that I have given the name "new creation millennialism." Chapters 2 and 3 will lay out the insuperable difficulties that are faced by historic premillennialism and amillennialism, respectively. Chapter 4 will present a rebuttal to key amillennial arguments against the possibility of a premillennial reading of Rev. 20:1-10. The Conclusion will sum up the gains made by the "new creation millennialism" approach and offer some theological reflections.

Readers should be aware that I have not composed *New Creation Millennialism* to be a full-scale scholarly offering. Think of it instead as an economical presentation of the main elements of a case. I have intentionally privileged conciseness over comprehensiveness, in the hope that a broader range of readers will find it accessible. For those who desire an in-depth technical literary-critical discussion and interaction with the views of Revelation scholars, I recommend my well-known monograph, *After the Thousand Years: Resurrection and Judgment in Revelation 20*.[1]

[1] JSNTSup, 70; Sheffield: Sheffield Academic Press, 1992. See also the article-length review of that study by amillennialist Revelation commentator G.K. Beale, "Review Article: J.W. Mealy *After the Thousand Years*," *EQ* 66 (3, 1994), 229-49, and see now J.W. Mealy, "Revelation is One: Revelation 20 and the Quest to Make the Scriptures Agree," in *Reconsidering the Relationship between Biblical and Systematic Theology in the New Testament* (ed. B.E. Reynolds, B. Lugioyo, and K.J. Vanhoozer; WUNT 2.369; Tübingen: Mohr Siebeck, 2014), 131-53. The latter article contains my rebuttal of Beale's main criticisms of *After the Thousand Years* and a critique of Beale's own interpretation of Revelation 20 (as showcased in Beale's *The Book of Revelation: A Commentary on the Greek Text* [NIGTC; Grand Rapids: Eerdmans, Carlisle: Paternoster Press, 1999]). Further on this, see Chapter 3, below, esp. 100-105.

Chapter 1
Exposition of Rev. 19:5–21:8

Rev. 19:5–21:8—Narrative Context, or the Story So Far

In terms of immediate context, Rev. 19:5 transitions to a new episode in John's vision narrative. The previous episode, Rev. 17:1–19:4, has revealed "the judgment of the great prostitute" (17:1), also identified as "Babylon the Great" (17:5). In John's vision, the drunken prostitute empress Babylon personifies a city-empire that dominates the whole world through its wealth and economic power (17:15, 18; 18:3, 9-10, 23). In the same way that the "beast" of Revelation 13 functions as a kind of counterfeit Christ, so Babylon functions as a counterfeit New Jerusalem. Indeed, the beast and the Great City (18:10, 19) show themselves to be the opposite of their counterparts, persecuting and murdering those who follow Christ and those who speak the truth on behalf of God (11:3-8; 13:7-17; 17:6; 18:24; cf. Dan. 7:21, 25).

Looking further back in the story, in Revelation 12 we read of a great war in heaven, which results in the expulsion of the devil and the angels loyal to him (12:7-9; cf. 12:4). At this, a triumphant voice in heaven proclaims, "Now have come the salvation and the power and the kingdom of our God and the authority of his Messiah" (12:10),[1] suggesting that this moment

[1] Quotations from the Bible, unless otherwise stated, are from the New Revised Standard Version Bible, copyright © 1989 the Division of Christian Education of the National Council of the Churches of Christ in the United States of America. Used by permission. All rights reserved.

of expulsion represents a kind of "beginning of the end" for the devil and all his minions. As though to confirm this, we then hear that the devil, for the moment at liberty on the earth, is enraged because he "knows that his time is short" (12:12). We are given clues that this short time, during which he will "make war on…those who keep the commandments of God and hold the testimony of Jesus" (12:17), lasts three and a half years (compare 12:6, 14). We are promptly introduced (13:1) to "the beast," whose devil-empowered career of deadly persecution against followers of Jesus lasts, not coincidentally, 42 months (13:5; cf. 11:2-3).

The close association in activity (intense persecution of the faithful) and duration of activity (three and a half years) between the devil and the beast, his false Christ (13:2), creates a strong expectation that the two of them will experience some kind of radical disempowerment *at the same moment.* Those of John's readers who are familiar with Daniel 7, with its depiction of the three-and-a-half-year persecuting career and fiery destruction of the fourth beast (Dan. 7:11-14; 21-22; 25-27; 12:7, 11-12) will suspect that the beast is to be *destroyed by fire* at the end of this period, and this expectation will later be strengthened by Rev. 17:8, 11. But what is to become of the devil, when the career that he shares with his surrogate comes to an end? Nothing in Daniel or in the Revelation narrative prior to Rev. 20:1-3 gives a hint as to what exactly will happen to him when his time is up. The fact that he is enraged by the knowledge that "his time is short" (12:12) does, however, suggest that he expects to lose whatever power and freedom he has when his time runs out.

After the readers are introduced in Revelation 13 to the beast, and warned of his demand for worship by all human beings on earth, to be enforced with deadly force (13:8, 12, 16-17), Revelation 14 and 15 proceed with scenes of warning and promise—warning to the readers that capitulating to the beast's demand for worship will result in fiery punishment when Christ comes in glory, and promise to the readers that if they remain faithful to death they will find safety, rest, and even triumph beyond death (esp. 14:6-13). Revelation 16 narrates a vision in which seven angels pour out on the earth "the seven bowls of the wrath of God" (16:1). In the midst of this we hear of a bowl of God's wrath targeting "the beast's kingdom" (16:10). This suggests that the beast, whose "number is the number of a man" (13:18), is to be understood as an individual person with a home country which, under his leadership, operates as a world empire (cf. Rev. 13:14-17; Dan. 3:1-6).

In Revelation 17, we meet the beast's capital city, Babylon. Babylon is pictured as a drunken empress who rides the beast (17:3). This image suggests a paradoxical relationship in which she believes she is controlling him, but he, being a *beast*, a wild animal (Gr. θηρίον), is in fact uncontrollable, and will take her wherever he wishes. In fact, like a wild animal, he will ultimately turn on her, betraying her to her enemies, who, in league with him, will "devour her flesh and burn her up with fire" (17:16-18). This stark prediction seems to be associated with the end of the beast's career and Christ's coming in glory (cf. 16:12-14; 17:12-14; 19:19-21).

Revelation 18 (more precisely, 18:1–19:4) follows immediately upon the prediction of Babylon's betrayal by the beast, and dramatizes the tale of her fiery demise by describing it from multiple viewpoints—angelic, heavenly, and human. In this multiple telling, we learn of her status as the wealthiest (18:14-19; cf. 17:4), the most powerful (18:3, 10, 18, 23; cf. 17:18), and the most murderous (18:24; cf. 17:6) empire on earth.

Thus run the large lines of narrative progress between Rev. 12:1 and 19:4. To summarize the "state of play" at the juncture between 19:4 and 19:5, we can observe that a number of questions remain up in the air, in terms of events that the readers (or hearers) will have been led to anticipate. For example:

- Does the "one hour" of collusion between the beast and the kings of the east, which results in Babylon's destruction (17:12-17), come at the very end of the beast's three-and-a-half-year career?
- Are we soon to see the "battle of Harmagedon," which explicitly involves the beast and the kings of the east, as well as "the kings of the whole world" (16:12-16)?
- Are we soon to see the "destruction" that awaits the beast (17:8, 11), and the coming on the clouds of the "One like a Human Being," as in Dan. 7:11-14?

- What is to become of the devil, when, at the same time as the beast's career comes to a close, his own freedom comes to an end (12:13-17)?

These are some of the expectations—or at least questions—that the process of reading the text of Revelation will have generated by the time readers encounter the nineteenth chapter. Because there have already been many intimations of and symbolic representations of the Parousia,[2] interleaved with scenes of judgment, warning, and encouragement, the readers will not have a basis to be confident as to what will be revealed next after 19:4. But they will have a sense of forward momentum and suspense. A number of hints have signaled a coming denouement (especially the sixth and seventh seals, trumpets, and bowls) in which there will be a final confrontation between God, his Christ, and the faithful on the one hand, and the angelic and human forces of wickedness on this earth on the other hand. In this battle, however, they will know that the victory absolutely belongs to God, to Christ, and to the faithful (e.g. 2:25-28; 6:15-17; 11:15-19; 17:12-14).

Rev. 19:5–21:8
Brief Remarks on Composition and Structure

Rev. 19:5-10 announces a great and glorious wedding. The Groom is the Lamb, Jesus Christ, and his Bride is the community of the faithful, the saints.

The vision of Rev. 19:11-21 is devoted to the royal *Groom*, pictured as the warrior-king who triumphs over the murderous would-be usurper, the beast. The theme of the royal Groom as a triumphant warrior finds solid OT roots in Psalm 45. Correspondingly, Rev. 21:1-7 (and, indeed, the larger section 21:1–22:5)[3] is devoted to the *Bride*, who comes down from heaven arrayed in splendor on her wedding day.

[2] The term "Parousia" does not itself occur in the Book of Revelation. It nonetheless serves as useful shorthand for the repeatedly narrated coming of God and Jesus Christ to judge the living and the dead and to rule on the earth.
[3] For the sake of brevity, I will end my exposition at Rev. 21:8. After a final warning in Rev. 21:8 about behavior that will result in a person being

Rev. 20:1-15, the section that comes between Rev. 19:11-21 and 21:1-7, is made up of two interlocking sections: 20:1-3 + 20:7-10 and 20:4-6 + 20:11-15 (see Figure 1 on p. 83 below, and the remarks associated with it). This central section of Rev. 20:1-15, in addition to wrapping up the story of the final defeat and destruction of Satan, implicitly concerns itself with the third familiar element of a wedding: the *guests*. It elaborates on the question of *who* is invited to Christ's wedding, *on what basis* will some be invited and others not, and *what will ultimately happen* to those not invited. There is, of course, a compound metaphor operating here, given that the guests and the bride are both to be understood as symbols for the same faithful community. The invited guests, however, represent that community under its individual aspect, whereas the bride represents the community under its corporate aspect. Throughout Revelation we see equal attention being given to *individual* and *corporate* perspectives, whether it be in relation to promise, accountability, judgment, or reward.

Exposition of Rev. 19:5-21

Introductory Remarks on Rev. 19:5-21

Starting with Rev. 19:5, nearly everything said until 19:21 is going to link in some way with previous *visions* of the Parousia in Revelation, previous *promises* associated with the Parousia in Revelation, or previous *references* to the Parousia in Revelation. It will become clear as we go along that John's way of telling his visions creates not a one-dimensional narrative *thread*, but rather a two-dimensional or multi-dimensional narrative *fabric*, whose structure is achieved by the constant inweaving of cross-references—to previous passages in Revelation, to the visions of OT prophets, and to the traditional words of Jesus. I will now develop my exposition by presenting short textual sections and offering observations and comments.

excluded from the new creation and consigned to the pool of fire (cf. 20:10, 15), everything through 22:5 gives further elaboration to 21:1-2, without raising any new and significant issues in relation to the central argument being presented here.

Rev. 19:5

5 And from the throne came a voice saying,
"Praise our God, all you his servants,
and all who fear him, small and great."

Who is speaking here? Probably one or all of the "four living creatures," who are intimately associated with God's throne, both in Revelation and in Ezekiel (see Ezek. 1:4-28; 10:1-22; Rev. 4:6-8). Mention of God's "servants," "the small and the great," serves to recall the Parousia announcement by the "24 elders" after the sounding of the seventh trumpet:[4]

Rev. 11:17-18

17 We give you thanks, Lord God Almighty,
who are and who were,[5]
for you have taken your great power
and begun to reign.
18 The nations raged,
but your wrath has come,
and the time for judging the dead,
for rewarding **your servants**, the prophets
and saints and all who fear your name,
both small and great,
and for destroying those who destroy the earth.

[4] There are many indications that the seventh trumpet scene (Rev. 11:15-19) represents the Parousia, among which are these: (1) an angel swears in 10:5-7 that in the days of the seventh trumpet "there will be no more delay"; (2) the seventh trumpet scene opens with an announcement that God and his Christ have assumed the rulership of the world (v. 15), and this is repeated in v. 17; (3) it is the time for the dead to be judged (v. 18); (4) it is the time for a great confrontation between God and the nations, who are "enraged" (cf. Ps. 2:1 LXX, Rev. 16:14; 17:14; 19:17-21); (5) it is time for rewards to be given out to the faithful (v. 18), as in many of the letters to the seven churches; and (6) it ends (v. 19) with a description of the dramatic opening of heaven (cf. Rev. 19:11) to reveal "the ark of the covenant," a symbol for God's throne (cf. Exod. 25:18-22; 1 Sam. 4:4; 2 Sam. 6:2; 2 Kgs 19:15; 1 Chron. 13:6; Ps. 80:1; 99:1; Isa. 37:16; Ezek. 10:1), followed by words that recall the climax of the seventh seal scene (cf. Rev. 8:5; 11:18).
[5] Lit. "the Is and the Was." See Rev. 1:8; 4:8.

Rev. 19:6-7a

> 6Then I heard what seemed to be the voice of a great multitude, like the sound of many waters[6] and like the sound of mighty thunderpeals, crying out,
>
> "Hallelujah!
> For the Lord our God
> the Almighty reigns.
> 7Let us rejoice and exult
> and give him the glory…"

The "great multitude," whose collective voice is as awesome as all the loudest noises known to most people in the ancient world—waterfall, thunder, and pounding waves—recalls the "great multitude" that welcomed God and the Lamb with praise and glory at their Parousia in 7:9-17.[7] The sound of their voice also recalls the singing and harp-playing "like the sound of many waters and like the sound of loud thunder" that celebrated of the Parousia of the Lamb in 14:2.[8]

[6] A waterfall, or perhaps a deafening downpour? See Ezek. 1:24; 43:2.

[7] There are a number of indications which, in combination, serve to give us confidence that the "great multitude" scene (Rev. 7:9-17) represents the Parousia. Among them are these: (1) the participants wear white. The white clothes recall the promise in Rev. 3:4-5 that the overcomers would walk with Jesus in white, and most of the promises to overcomers in the letters to the seven churches concern blessings they will experience when he comes. (2) They wave palm branches, which, in addition to being familiar symbols of victory, also recall the crowd's greeting of Jesus during his triumphal entry to Jerusalem (Mt. 21:8-9 || Mk 11:8-10 || Lk. 19:36-38 || Jn 12:12-16). (3) The promise that these veterans of the great tribulation (7:13-14) will never hunger or thirst links both to the promise to the overcomers in Ephesus that they will have access to the tree of life (2:7), and to the mention in Rev. 7:17 of springs of living water, which will be echoed in the Parousia promise of Rev. 22:17. (4) The statement that "the Lamb at the center of the throne will be their shepherd" (7:17) will be echoed in the Parousia promise of Rev. 22:12, via Isa. 40:10-11.

[8] The following considerations combine to indicate that Rev. 14:1-5 is a Parousia scene. (1) Mount Zion (see v. 1) is associated in OT prophecy with the Parousia of God as Judge and Savior (cf. Isa. 59:20, quoted by Paul in reference to Jesus in Rom. 11:26-27; Joel 2:32; Obad. 1:17-21), and in Revelation, God's Parousia is always identical with Jesus' Parousia (see nt. 31 below). (2) The paradoxical reference to Jesus as the Lamb who is also the Shepherd links 14:4 to 7:17 (see nt. 7 above), which itself follows on the heels

Rev. 19:7b-8

> 7 …for the marriage of the Lamb has come,
> and his bride has made herself ready;
> 8 to her it has been granted to be clothed
> with fine linen, bright and pure"—
> for the fine linen is the righteous deeds of the saints.[9]

In the Gospels, Jesus seems to use the idea of a wedding—at which he is the groom—as a parabolic way of talking about his future coming in glory, i.e. his Parousia (Mt. 22:1-14; 25:1-10).[10] The more filled-out idea that Jesus is the Groom and the community of his faithful followers are the Bride is familiar from a number of Pauline passages (2 Cor. 11:2; Gal. 4:26; Eph. 5:30-32).[11] The idea of the wedding day between Christ and his church in fact seems an entirely fitting metaphor for his Parousia, the long-hoped-for day of their eternal union.[12]

Rev. 19:9-10

> 9 And the angel said to me, "Write this: Blessed are those who are invited to the marriage supper of the Lamb." And he said to me, "These are true words of God." 10 Then I fell down at his feet to worship him, but he said to me, "You must not do that! I am a fellow servant with you and your comrades who hold the testimony of Jesus.

of the scene of the sealing of the 144,000. (3) Reference to the 144,000 as "firstfruits" to God and the Lamb (14:4) brings in the theme of the harvest, a familiar metaphor for the end of the age and the Parousia (e.g. Mt. 3:12; 13:30, 39; Rev. 14:14-16).

[9] The Greek word δικαιώματα (from δικαίωμα) here doesn't really mean, as most translations render it, "righteous deeds." It means legal proofs in favor of someone's case in court. It's true that righteous acts serve as evidence in God's court, but the legal meaning is lost when the word is under-translated as "righteous deeds."

[10] John the Baptist and Jesus both picture Jesus as a groom without making explicit who or what the bride might be (Mt. 9:15; 22:1-14; 25:1-10; Mk. 2:19-20; Lk. 5:35; Jn 3:29).

[11] "Ephesians" was very probably addressed to Laodicea, which, like Ephesus, was also one of the seven churches to which Revelation was addressed (cf. Col. 4:16).

[12] For OT background to this concept, see Isa. 54:5; 62:4-5. Psalm 45 also provides interesting background here, with its celebration of both the king's wedding and his glorious victory in battle (see the nearby Rev. 19:11-21).

> Worship God! For the testimony of Jesus is the spirit of prophecy."[13]

Note the compound metaphor here—the faithful of God and of Jesus are not only the Bride, but also the wedding guests. Jesus used this concept (worthy guests at a wedding feast) to teach about the coming of the Kingdom of God, which event is identical with his Parousia (Mt. 22:1-14).

Rev. 19:11-12

> 11 Then I saw heaven opened, and there was a white horse! Its rider is called Faithful and True,[14] and in righteousness he judges and makes war. 12 His eyes are like a flame of fire,[15] and on his head are many diadems; and he has a name inscribed that no one knows but himself.

The opening of heaven recalls two previous Parousia scenes: the sixth seal (see 6:14) and the seventh trumpet (see 11:19). The white horse (cf. 6:1) symbolizes Christ's victorious conquest, which we are about to witness in 19:19-21.[16] The rider is obviously Jesus, who called himself "the Holy One, the True One" in Rev. 3:7 and "the faithful and true witness" in Rev. 3:14 (see also "the faithful witness" in Rev. 1:5). See also, for OT background, Ps. 96:13, which prophesies the coming of God as faithful and just judge of the world. In Revelation, Jesus as Messiah always joins God in carrying out the eschatological

[13] It appears that John may be having a hard time distinguishing between the angel and Jesus (see Rev. 1:1-2; 22:8-9). The angel is saying that all he is doing is speaking God's words, or, in other words, prophesying. And he's saying that to present the testimony of/about Jesus (as John and many Christians have faithfully done) is no less prophetic. He looks upon John as an equal and a colleague, and he wants John to look upon him as an equal and a colleague.

[14] Some mss leave out the word "called."

[15] For the description, see Dan. 7:9; 10:6; Rev. 1:15; 2:18.

[16] The rider of Rev. 6:1 is successful in his military conquests, but he is *not* to be understood as Jesus. The first six seals reveal various aspects of and results of human sinfulness: aggressive war and imperial conquest, 6:1-2; insurrection and murder, 6:3-4; economic injustice, 6:5-6; violence, famines, plagues, incursion of wild animals (deadly conditions that attend external and internal wars), 6:7-8; persecution of those faithful to God, 6:9-11; and hostility and fearfulness towards God, 6:12-17.

judgments and the eschatological reign prophesied in the OT (e.g. Rev. 6:16-17; 11:15; 12:10; 14:9-10; 19:15). John's vision of "many diadems," which is to say, many *royal crowns*, implies that Jesus has authority to rule all the nations of the world (not just Judah/Israel), and perhaps all realms of creation whatsoever. The mysterious "names" inscribed on the crowns would thus be *titles* that relate to realms of his authority that are beyond human comprehension.

Rev. 19:13-15

> 13 He is clothed in a robe dipped[17] in blood, and his name is called The Word of God. 14 And the armies of heaven, wearing fine linen, white and pure, were following him on white horses. 15 From his mouth comes a sharp sword with which to strike down the nations, and he will rule[18] them with a rod of iron; he will tread the wine press of the fury of the wrath of God the Almighty.

Christ's blood-drenched robe recalls both his own sacrificial death and the oracle of God's Parousia as warrior-judge in Isa. 63:1-6 (quoting here vv. 1-3):

Isa. 63:1-3

> 1 "Who is this that comes from Edom,
> from Bozrah in garments stained crimson?
> Who is this so splendidly robed,
> marching in his great might?"
> "It is I, announcing vindication, mighty to save."
> 2 "Why are your robes red,
> and your garments like theirs who tread the wine press?"
> 3 "I have trodden the wine press alone,
> and from the peoples no one was with me;
> I trod them in my anger
> and trampled them in my wrath;
> their juice spattered on my garments,
> and stained all my robes."

[17] Or "drenched in"; lit. "dunked in." Some mss have "sprinkled with."
[18] Lit. "shepherd."

The name/title "Word of God" (19:13) of course identifies this as Jesus (Jn 1:1-18). The "armies of heaven" that follow Jesus may considered to be angels[19] or to include angels, but it is probable that they to be recognized above all as his faithful human followers. After all, (1) they are riding white horses, which symbolize victory, (2) Jesus has promised his faithful ones, whom he calls "conquerors" or "victorious warriors" in the letters to the angels of the seven churches, that they will be rewarded with the privilege of joining him at his Parousia in smashing the sinful nations of the world like so much pottery (cf. Ps. 2:9; Rev. 2:25-26; 17:14), and (3) they are wearing bright, white, clean garments, another reward that Jesus has promised to give his faithful ones when he comes (Rev. 3:4-5; cf. 19:8). The violence of this imagery is recast in a new light by John's vision of the sword coming from Christ's mouth, as he also saw in his very first vision of him (Rev. 1:16; cf. Rev. 2:12, 16; Isa. 49:2; Hos. 6:5). The only weapon Jesus needs in order to defeat his enemies is the power of his truthful testimony (Rev. 19:21). Like the sharp sword, the "iron staff" of 19:14 also has OT prophetic roots and has been associated with the Parousia of Jesus earlier in Revelation (see Isa. 11:4; Rev. 2:27; 12:5).

Rev. 19:16

> 16 On his robe and on his thigh he has a name inscribed, "King of kings and Lord of lords."

The phrase "King of Kings and Lord of Lords" is not only an appropriate title for the Messiah of all humanity, but it is also a divine title (1 Tim. 6:15; cf. Dan. 2:47). As with so many other titles and attributes, it has been ascribed to Jesus earlier in Revelation in the context of a Parousia prediction (Rev. 17:14).

Rev. 19:17-18

> 17 Then I saw an angel standing in the sun, and with a loud voice he called to all the birds that fly in midheaven, "Come, gather for the great supper of God, 18 to eat the

[19] The following passages might tend to suggest that angels are in view: Deut. 33:2; Ps. 68:17; *1 Enoch* 1:9; Mt. 16:27; 25:31; Mk 8:38; Lk. 9:26; 2 Thess. 1:7-8; Jude 1:14; Rev. 5:11.

> flesh of kings, the flesh of captains, the flesh of the mighty, the flesh of horses and their riders—flesh of all, both free and slave, both small and great."

These verses contain a cross-reference to Ezek. 39:17-20, an oracle of the great battle in which God defeats the enemies of Israel and inaugurates the age of Messiah.[20] The reference to all military and social classes here in Rev. 19:18 serves to recall not only the similar list of classes of people who served the beast (cf. 13:16, and immediately below, v. 19), but even more pointedly the list of classes of people who fled from the Parousia of God and Jesus Christ in Rev. 6:15: "the kings of the earth and the magnates and the generals and the rich and the powerful, and everyone, slave and free."[21]

Rev. 19:19-21

> 19 Then I saw the beast and the kings of the earth with their armies gathered to make war against the rider on the horse and against his army. 20 And the beast was captured, and with it the false prophet who had performed in its presence the signs[22] by which he deceived those who had received the mark of the beast and those who worshiped its image. These two were thrown alive into the lake of fire that burns with sulfur. 21 And the rest were killed by the sword of the rider on the horse, the sword that came from his mouth; and all the birds were gorged with their flesh.

Owing to the multiple Psalm 2 references the readers have encountered in Revelation (2:26-27; 11:18; 12:5; 19:15), they will find this scene instantly and unmistakably identifiable as a vision of the confrontation anticipated in that Psalm:

[20] For the connection between Ezek. 39 and the inauguration of the messianic age prophesied in Ezek. 36, note the following connections: Ezek. 39:26 = 34:23-24, 28; 37:24; Ezek. 39:27 = 37:21, 25; Ezek. 39:29 = 36:25-27; 37:23.

[21] In other words everybody, from the very top to the very bottom of the social ladder.

[22] In other words, miracles that the false prophet would have performed to attest to the beast's divine authority.

Psalm 2:1-3, 7-9[23]

1 Why do the nations conspire,[24]
and the peoples plot in vain?
2 The kings of the earth set themselves,
and the rulers take counsel together,
against the LORD and his anointed, saying,
3 "Let us burst their bonds asunder,
and cast their cords from us."
. . .
7 I will tell of the decree of the LORD:
He said to me, "You are my son;
today I have begotten you.
8 Ask of me, and I will make the nations your heritage,
and the ends of the earth your possession.
9 You shall break them with a rod of iron,
and dash them in pieces like a potter's vessel."

Rev. 19:19-21 thus describes a decisive and final confrontation between Jesus, followed by his armies, and the beast, followed by "the kings of the earth" and their armies. This confrontation, alluded to briefly in Rev. 11:18, and there associated with the judgment of the dead and the rewarding of all the faithful, had also been predicted in Revelation 16:13-16 and 17:11-14. Each of these deserves to be quoted in full:

Rev. 16:13-16

13 And I saw three foul spirits like frogs coming from the mouth of the dragon, from the mouth of the beast, and from the mouth of the false prophet. 14 These are demonic spirits, performing signs, who go abroad to the kings of the whole world, to assemble them for battle on the great

[23] This Psalm is alluded to or quoted numerous times elsewhere in the NT as referring to Jesus as the king described in the divine voice as "my Son" (Mt. 3:17; 17:5; Mk 1:11; 9:7; Lk. 3:22; 9:35; Jn 1:49; Acts 4:25-27; 13:33; Heb. 1:2, 5; 5:5).

[24] Rev. 11:18 follows the Hebrew of Ps. 2:1, which has the word *ragash* which is interpreted as meaning "rage," rather than "conspire," so that God and the nations are seen as *enraged with one another* (see τὰ ἔθνη ὠργίσθησαν καὶ ἦλθεν ἡ ὀργή σου, "the nations raged and your wrath came," Rev. 11:18; cf. Ps. 2:1, 5, 11).

> day of God the Almighty. 15 ("See, I am coming like a thief![25] Blessed is the one who stays awake and is clothed, not going about naked and exposed to shame."[26]) 16 And they assembled them at the place that in Hebrew is called Harmagedon.

Rev. 17:11-14

> 11 As for the beast that was and is not, it is an eighth but it belongs to the seven, and it goes to destruction. 12 And the ten horns that you saw are ten kings who have not yet received a kingdom, but they are to receive authority as kings for one hour, together with the beast. 13 These are united in yielding their power and authority to the beast; 14 they will make war on the Lamb, and the Lamb will conquer them, for he is Lord of lords and King of kings, and those with him are called and chosen and faithful.

These two passages make it clear that Satan, the beast, and the false prophet are all collaborators in an all-out resistance to the coming of Jesus as Lord and Ruler of the earth (16:13-14). John's readers know that the career of the beast *began* when Satan recruited the beast, and a three-and-a-half year timer began to wind down on Satan's last season of freedom.[27] The end of the beast's career thus signals the end of the three and a half years (13:5) and the end of Satan's "short" rampage (12:12). This logic leads us, when we see the beast and the false prophet captured and destroyed in Rev. 19:19-20, to expect that Satan himself will be defeated and that his freedom will be taken away. This expectation is immediately fulfilled in Rev. 20:1-3, in which John sees Satan captured and banished from the earth to the prison of the abyss.

[25] See Mt. 24:42-44; Lk. 12:35-40; Rev. 3:3.
[26] Lit. "naked, and they see his disarray." Having your clothes in "disarray" is a euphemism for exposing yourself. In times of danger, the wise person goes to bed with their robe belted, ready to get up in an emergency.
[27] This time period is also expressed equivalently as 1,260 days (three and a half 360-day Roman years) and as 42 months: see Rev. 12:6, 14; 13:5; cf. also 11:2-3; Dan. 7:25; 12:7.

Exposition of Rev. 20:1-10

Rev. 20:1-3

> 1 Then I saw an angel coming down from heaven, holding in his hand the key to the bottomless pit and a great chain. 2 He seized the dragon, that ancient serpent,[28] who is the Devil and Satan, and bound him for a thousand years, 3 and threw him into the pit, and locked and sealed it over him, so that he would deceive the nations no more, until the thousand years were ended. After that he must be let out for a little while.

Satan's freedom is now completely taken away—he is not only imprisoned, but chained up ("bound") within his locked and sealed prison. But we are warned that another brief period of freedom lies in the distant future for him. Is there any scriptural precedent for the idea that the devil will be captured and imprisoned—but not destroyed—at the end of the current age, only to be released for final judgment much later (see Rev. 20:7-10)? Without a doubt, this idea finds specific OT roots in the oracle that ends Isaiah 24:

Isa. 24:21-23

> 21 On that day the LORD will punish
> the host of heaven in heaven,
> and on earth the kings of the earth.
> 22 They will be gathered together
> like prisoners in a pit;
> they will be shut up in a prison,
> and after many days they will be punished.
> 23 Then the moon will be abashed,
> and the sun ashamed;
> for the LORD of hosts will reign
> on Mount Zion and in Jerusalem,
> and before his elders he will manifest his glory.

[28] See Gen. 3:1-15; Isa. 27:1.

We have just seen "the kings of the earth"[29] slain in Rev. 19:19-21, which, according to the worldview of Revelation, results in their being sent to Hades, the prison of the underworld.[30] Satan and his angels once belonged to the "host [i.e. *army*] of heaven" (cf. Rev. 19:14, 19), but they rebelled and were defeated, and were thereafter locked out of heaven (Rev. 12:7-9). Now that Jesus Christ has come to reign on earth (which in Revelation *always* equals God's coming to reign),[31] we see Satan being captured and imprisoned in the underworld along with the kings of the earth (see Isa. 24:22 above). Satan's angelic followers are implicitly consigned to the same fate, just as the followers of the beast and false prophet, characterized as "the kings of the earth and their armies" in 19:19, are all slain and sent to the underworld ("the rest were killed by the sword that came from his mouth," 19:21). In 20:4-6, of course, we are going to see a depiction of the reign of Christ, which corresponds to Isa. 24:23 above. The strong linkage between Isa. 24:21-23 (and indeed the whole oracle of Isaiah 24–27) and Revelation 20 will become absolutely unmistakable when we look at Rev. 20:7-10 below.[32]

[29] The universality of this expression is underlined by the parallel expression οἱ βασιλεῖς τῆς οἰκουμένης ὅλης, "the kings of the whole world" (16:14).
[30] In the vision of Rev. 6:8, when Death goes out, Hades follows him to collect the people that he slays. "Hades" (Gr. ᾅδης, Rev. 1:18; 6:8; 20:13, 15; cf. Mt. 11:23; Lk. 10:15; 16:23; Acts 2:27, 31) and "the abyss" (Gr. ἄβυσσος: Rev. 9:1, 2, 11; 11:7; 17:8; 20:1, 3; cf. Lk. 8:31; Rom. 10:7) can both equally refer to the underworld where dead people are conceived of as being trapped (Rom. 10:7; Rev. 11:7; 17:8). On the other hand, angelic/demonic spirits including the devil are always spoken of as trapped in the abyss, and not Hades. The distinction seems to be terminological rather than cosmological. The spirits of the dead and the rebellious angelic spirits are sent to the same place.
[31] See Rev. 2:26-27; 3:21; 5:13; 6:16-17; 7:15-17; 11:15-18; 12:10; 16:14-16; 19:6-9, 15-16; 20:6; 21:22-23; 22:3-4, 12 (see Isa. 40:10; 62:11).
[32] Note that Isa. 24:21-23 comes as the climax of a chapter that envisions the complete destruction of the physical world and the final demise of humanity—which humanity effectively brings upon itself (Isa. 24:1-22, esp. vv. 3-6, 18-20; cf. Rev. 11:18f; 16:8-9). In the Book of Revelation the Parousia alone corresponds to this total crisis, therefore any attempt to read a temporal recapitulation in Rev. 20:1-3 will create a clash between Revelation and one of its most important OT prophetic background texts.

Rev. 20:4-5

> 4 Then I saw thrones, and those seated on them were given authority to judge.[33] I also saw the souls of those who had been beheaded for their testimony to Jesus and for the word of God. They[34] had not worshiped the beast or its image and had not received its mark on their foreheads or their hands. They came to life[35] and reigned with Christ a thousand years. 5 (The rest of the dead did not come to life[36] until the thousand years were ended.) This is the first resurrection.

The first two sentences here immediately cross-reference this vision with the vision of Daniel 7, which narrates the Parousia of God and of the One Like a Human Being (traditionally, *the Son of Man*). In that vision, thrones are set up, and God takes his seat as Judge along with a panel of divinely appointed judges or jurors (Dan. 7:9-10). The divine court makes its decision, and the "fourth beast," understood to represent the final evil empire of this age, is destroyed and its body consigned to fire (Dan. 7:7, 11 || Rev. 18:8 || 19:20), and a human figure, representing God's saints, receives the kingdom forever: "for the age, and for the ages of the ages" (Dan. 7:13-14, 18 || Rev. 20:4; 22:5). The reason why the court sits and decrees the destruction of the beast is that it has been murderously—and successfully—attacking the saints (Dan. 7:21-22, 25-27 || Rev. 12:17; 13:7; 19:20; 20:4). The evidence is simply rock-solid that John understands himself to be describing the same Parousia and judgment scene in Rev. 20:4 as Daniel described in Daniel 7.[37]

The fact that *resurrection* is the outcome for the faithful who have not given in and worshipped the beast coheres with Jesus' promise in the letter to the angel of the Ephesus: "Be faithful

[33] Lit. "and judgment was given to them." This phrase (Gr. καὶ κρίμα ἐδόθη αὐτοῖς) can also mean "and judgment was passed in their favor."

[34] Or "and whoever."

[35] Or "And they lived."

[36] Lit. "didn't live."

[37] Secondary matters needn't detain us here, such as the fact that John sees the last king of the fourth empire (the "little horn" of Dan. 7:8, 21) under the figures of the beast (Rev. 13:1-7; 17:3, 8) and one of the heads of the beast (Rev. 17:9-11).

until death, and I will give you the crown of life" (Rev. 2:10). It also coheres with the fact that throughout the New Testament the hope of resurrection for believers is solidly linked to the Parousia of Jesus. In Revelation, in fact, the Parousia is the repeatedly emphasized time for *all* rewards to be given to the faithful (cf. 2:7, 10, 17,[38] 25-28;[39] 3:4-5, 11-12, 21; 11:18; 19:9; 20:6; 21:6-7; 22:1-5, 12, 14, 17), and *Rev. 20:4 is the one and only place in Revelation where John explicitly describes the granting of this most important of all rewards.*

It is noteworthy that John very carefully phrases himself in Rev. 20:4 so that he does *not* say that only those killed by the beast will take part in the thousand-year reign with Christ. First he supplements his reference to those killed by the beast with the phrase "and whoever had not worshiped the beast or its image and had not received its mark on their foreheads or their hands," then he uses the Greek verb ἔζησαν, which can equally be taken to mean "they lived" or "they came to life."[40] He is consciously opening the door to the possibility—also anticipated by Jesus and Paul[41]—that some of the faithful will survive until Jesus comes in glory.

It is worth noting again that John *does not* say that the saints will stop reigning with Christ when the thousand years (a nice, round period for an age to last)[42] are completed, but only that

[38] The hidden manna is of course Jesus himself, the food of eternal life (cf. Jn 6:48-51), whom the faithful will receive when he comes.
[39] The morning star (Rev. 2:28) is also none other than Jesus himself, whom the faithful will receive when he comes (cf. Rev. 22:16).
[40] The verb ἔζησαν is the aorist tense-form of ζάω, "to live." It can be taken either as a simple aorist (equivalent to an English simple preterit) or as an ingressive aorist, which would convey the idea that the verbal action began or started. By contrast, when John speaks in 20:5 of the "rest of the dead" coming back to life, he uses the verb ἀναζάω, which cannot be taken to mean simply "live," but must mean "come to life again."
[41] See Mt. 24:31; Mk 13:27; 1 Cor. 15:52; 1 Thess. 4:15-17 (but see also Mt. 24:22; Mk 13:20 for the remoteness of this possibility).
[42] Pseudo-Barnabas, for example, who writes nearly contemporaneously with John and does not seem to be aware of the Book of Revelation, speaks of the present world being divided into six thousand-year periods which are God's days, as in Ps. 90:4, and he speaks of the first "day" of the new creation as also being a thousand-year period (Ep. Barn. 6:18-19, see pp. 151-153 below). Barnabas does not, however, use the word αἰών in this context.

they reign for that period and that Satan and the "rest of the dead" (v. 5) remain imprisoned in the underworld for that period.[43] As in Dan. 7:18, when the Son of Man (Rev. 1:13) comes in glory, the saints not only reign for the age that his coming inaugurates (Rev. 20:4, 6), but also for the ages upon ages that follow (Gr. εἰς τοὺς αἰῶνας τῶν αἰώνων, Rev. 22:5).[44]

Rev. 20:6

> 6 Blessed and holy are those who share in the first resurrection. Over these the second death has no power, but they will be priests of God and of Christ, and they will reign with him for a thousand years.[45]

Everything in this verse points to the Parousia some way. First, the "blessed" and "holy" status of the participants in the first resurrection cross-refers to Rev. 19:8-9, which interprets the sparkling clean wedding gown of the Lamb's bride as "the righteous deeds of the saints," which is to say, the *holy* ones,[46] and then immediately pronounces a *blessing* on those invited to the Lamb's wedding—a figure for the Parousia. Secondly, the statement that the participants in the first resurrection are invulnerable to "the second death" cross-refers to Jesus' promise in the letter to the angel of Ephesus that to those who remain faithful to death will receive the crown of (resurrection) Life and be invulnerable to the second death (Rev. 2:10-11). Promises in the

[43] In Rev. 1:18 Jesus says that he holds the keys of death and Hades. In saying this, Jesus implicitly affirms that Hades, the subterranean abode of the dead, is a prison from which he personally has the authority to free people (cf. Jn 5:25-29).

[44] The usual non-literal rendering of the expressions "for the age" and "for the age(s) of the ages" (in both Aramaic and Greek) as "forever" and "forever and ever" obscures both the presence and the significance of this parallel. For an introduction to the biblical conception of the past as a sequence of ages and the eschatological future as a never-ending sequence of ages, the first of which is the age to come—rather than the age to come being one undifferentiated and unending age—see J. Webb Mealy, *The End of the Unrepentant* (Eugene, OR: Wipf & Stock, 2014), 47-55, 139-49.

[45] NRSV follows uncials A and 051, which have "reign with him a thousand years," but I prefer the slightly-earlier-attested reading of uncials ℵ and 046, which have "reign with him for the thousand years."

[46] The same Greek adjective, ἅγιος, lies behind 19:8 and 20:6. It is used substantively in the first instance and attributively in the second.

seven letters are generally linked to the Parousia as the occasion for their fulfillment. Thirdly, the statement that the resurrected ones will be priests of God and Christ and rule with him cross-refers to the announcement in Rev. 5:10, "You have made them to be a kingdom and priests serving our God, and they will reign on earth."[47] The faithful already belong to Christ's kingdom and realm, and they already have a priestly identity, but the entirely logical moment for them to join Jesus *in ruling on the earth* is when he himself comes in glory to rule on the earth at his Parousia.

In Rev. 20:4-6 we have witnessed a judgment event that attends the Parousia of Jesus and which issues in resurrection for some—who have behaved worthily by remaining faithful to Jesus and refusing to worship the beast—and refusal of resurrection to "the rest of the dead" (v. 5). John explicitly speaks of this as "the first resurrection" (v. 6), and he immediately affirms of those who have a part in the first resurrection that "over these the second death has no power." The words of Jesus in Lk. 20:35 cohere closely with John's: "but those who are considered worthy of a place in that age and in the resurrection from the dead...cannot die anymore." John is saying here that the age to come, the age that follows the "judgment of the dead" at the Parousia (Rev. 11:18 || 20:4), lasts a thousand years,[48] and that those not found worthy of being raised for that age will eventually be raised after the completion of it—which is the same moment that Satan is going to be released from the prison of the underworld. John intentionally uses exactly the same phrase, "until the thousand years are completed" (Gr. ἄχρι τελεσθῇ τὰ χίλια ἔτη), to express the length of Satan's imprisonment in the underworld (20:3) and the length of the delay of the resurrection of the "rest of the dead" (20:5). The length of

[47] Some mss have "they reign on the earth," which seems to clash not only with the worldview of Revelation, but with that of the rest of the New Testament. This is not the age of earthly supremacy for the holy ones, but of service and witness in an often hostile world. On this see below, pp. 33-35.

[48] Nothing hangs on the question of whether John would have us take the thousand years literally as a specific and exact length of time. The point in any case is that a very long time in human terms (Ps. 90:4), which amounts to a whole age, will intervene between the resurrection of the holy ones (Rev. 20:4, 6) and that of the "rest of the dead" (20:5).

the *delay* in their resurrection amounts to the length of *their imprisonment* in the underworld of Hades (cf. Rev. 1:18).

Rev. 20:7-10

> 7 When the thousand years are ended, Satan will be released from his prison 8 and will come out to deceive the nations at the four corners of the earth, Gog and Magog, in order to gather them for battle;[49] they are as numerous as the sands of the sea.[50] 9 They marched up over the breadth of the earth[51] and surrounded the camp of the saints and the beloved city. And fire came down from heaven[52] and consumed them.[53] 10 And the devil who had deceived them was thrown into the lake of fire and sulfur, where the beast and the false prophet were, and they will be tormented day and night forever and ever.

Who are these "nations," whom Satan "goes out to deceive" when he is released from his underworld prison? They are, without a doubt, the "rest of the dead" (20:5) who are being resurrected. We know this for two reasons: (1) we know with certainty that they *cannot be* ordinary nations of mortals spared at the Parousia a thousand years previously (Rev. 6:13-14; 16:20; 19:21 etc.),[54] and (2) John has just given us a clear hint as to their identity by repeating in 20:5 the phrase "until the thousand years are completed" from 20:3. They have now been brought back to life, having also been released from the underworld—in their case, by resurrection.[55] The unrepentant of all

[49] Or "for the war."

[50] "Like the sand of the sea(shore) in number" is a common biblical expression for a huge, uncountable number (see Gen. 22:17; 32:12; Judg. 7:12; 1 Sam. 13:5; 1 Kgs 4:20; Isa. 10:22; Jer. 33:22; Heb. 11:12). Note also the cross-reference to Rev. 12:17 in this expression.

[51] See Hab. 1:6 for this imagery.

[52] Some mss. add "from God."

[53] For the biblical language of fire "consuming" those who attack the servant(s) of God, see 2 Kgs 1:10-14; Isa. 26:11; cf. Gen. 19:1-25.

[54] See the detailed demonstration of this below, pp. 47-53.

[55] John appears to supply a number of further clues that this is what he understands himself to be describing. For example: (1) In Revelation, the verb "to come up" or "to rise" (Gr. ἀναβαίνω) is used a number of times to describe

time, in a scene that cross-references Ezekiel's vision in Ezekiel 38:1-13, are sovereignly drawn out by God to see the peace, security, and prosperity of those redeemed by God (Ezek. 38:4, 8; Rev. 20:9). Rather than counting themselves blessed to be released from prison and granted resurrection life, they give themselves over to an attitude of envy, hostility, and murderous greed. They gather to attack the Beloved City, and are consumed by fire from heaven (20:8-9; cf. Ezek. 38:11-12, 19-23).

Whereas those blessed and holy ones who partook of the "first resurrection" arose to "a resurrection of life," these resurrected after the thousand years have been raised to "a resurrection of judgment" (Jn 5:28-29).[56] Those of the first resurrection were raised to "a resurrection of life" in the sense that they were raised for the purpose of giving them eternal life, because their lives of testimony to Jesus and God during their mortal lives proved them worthy of it.[57] Their resurrection was the *outcome*

beings coming up out of the sea or the earth or the bottomless pit—all three are realms of the dead (9:3; 11:7; 13:1; 13:11; 17:8). In particular, ἀναβαίνω is used to describe the beast "coming up" out of the sea and out of the bottomless pit in a counterfeit resurrection. Thus when John says in 20:9 that "they *came up* on the broad plain of the earth" (Gr. καὶ ἀνέβησαν ἐπὶ τὸ πλάτος τῆς γῆς), this can be taken as a hint that they were coming up from Hades, which lies beneath the surface of the earth. After all, you don't ordinarily "come up" onto the surface of a broad flat place. (Satan's underworld prison, correspondingly, is locked and sealed "over him," 20:3). (2) The phrase "the broad plain of the earth" (Gr. τὸ πλάτος τῆς γῆς) is rare, and occurs in the LXX of Dan. 12:1, where an angel speaks of the dead as those who "sleep *in* the broad plain of the earth," i.e. in their graves scattered throughout the earth. If they then come up *on* the broad plain the earth, they have left their graves to stand on the surface of the ground. (3) In Ezekiel, Gog's main hosts of Meshech and Tubal have previously been seen lying dead in the Pit, in Sheol (which the LXX translators uniformly render as Hades (Ezek. 32:25-27). This might have stood, in John's mind, as a clue that the attack of Gog and his hosts was an attack of the resurrected unrepentant.

[56] For a refutation of the notion that Jn 5:28-29 can only refer to a single general resurrection, see Mealy, *End of the Unrepentant* (see p. 29 nt. 44 above), 164-67. For Jesus, there is not simply one universal resurrection event that occurs at the end of time. For him, the "hour" (i.e. the appropriate season or moment) for resurrection "is now," beginning with his ministry, and it will last until every human being has been raised (Jn 5:25-29).

[57] Note that Jesus explicitly uses the language of worthiness in Rev. 3:4, as he does in Mt. 10:37-38; Lk. 20:35. Paul also is very comfortable using the

of the judgment that John saw in 20:4. The hordes of 20:8-9, on the other hand, having been judged at the same judgment (20:4) and found *unworthy* of resurrection and reign with Christ for the thousand years, are now raised after the completion of the thousand years "to a resurrection of judgment," in the sense that they are raised *for the purpose of judgment.* They have been raised for the purpose of evaluating them as to whether they will behave, upon their release from the prison of death, in a manner consistent with granting them unending life. They fail this final trial, and are condemned by their own actions to fiery destruction.[58]

This interpretation is dramatically confirmed by sixteen clear parallels between Revelation's final chapters and the extended oracle of Isaiah 24–27. For the sake of brevity, we will look at only two parallels here (in addition to Isa. 24:21-23, quoted above), but all sixteen parallels are presented for examination in Appendix 2.

Isa. 26:10-11

> 10 If favor is shown to the wicked,
> they do not learn righteousness;
> in the land of uprightness they deal perversely
> and do not see the majesty of the LORD.
> 11 O LORD, your hand is lifted up,
> but they do not see it.
> Let them see your zeal for your people, and be ashamed.
> Let the fire for your adversaries consume them.[59]

language of worthiness. See particularly, among many instances, Acts 13:46; 2 Thess. 1:5, 11.

[58] Those disinclined to allow the concept of a trial whose outcome is already foreknown ought to have equal trouble with the idea that the Book of Life (which stands open at the great judgment scene of Rev. 20:11-15) has been inscribed, and its exclusions have been determined, from the foundation of the world (Rev. 13:8; 17:8).

[59] LXX has, "O Lord, your arm is raised [to strike], and they have not noticed it. But when they do, they will be ashamed. Envy [or *jealousy*] will take hold of a people that has not learned [as contrasted with "the inhabitants of the earth learn righteousness," 26:10], and now fire will consume your adversaries."

The context for this section is that the earth and all of humanity has perished (Isa. 24:1-20), angelic and human authorities have been consigned to imprisonment *together* in the underworld (Isa. 24:21-22), and God has established his glorious reign on the earth with his capital in Jerusalem/Mt. Zion, granting everlasting life to his people (Isa. 24:23–26:8, esp. 25:8). What is the "favor" that is "shown to the wicked" (Isa. 26:10)? There are two natural answers to this: (1) God grants them grace, having mercifully chosen not to destroy them irrevocably for their past actions, and (2) God grants them the privilege of access to "the land of uprightness," which is to say, the land of God's Kingdom, the renewed, restored earth. Isaiah sees that "the wicked," having been granted mercy, are out to do something very wrong that involves a threat to God's people. Blinded by their own wickedness, they make the fateful mistake of misreading God's mercy towards them as inattention or lack of zeal for the safety of his people. Isaiah prays to God, "Let the fire for your adversaries consume them!" John in his vision narrative of Rev. 19:19–20:10 has re-created this entire narrative sequence. It is evident that he understands Isa. 26:10-11 as a picture of the deferred ("after many days") final judgment of those who had served a long, but nonetheless limited, imprisonment in the underworld in Isa. 24:22. John's vision in Rev. 20:9 thus pictures the answering of Isaiah's prayer in Isa. 26:11: "fire came down from heaven and consumed them."[60]

Isaiah presents another, more elaborate, version of this scenario (an unprovoked attack on the community of the faithful in the context of God's glorious kingdom) a few verses further on, right after he prophesies that the faithful will be resurrected and the oppressors will be left unresurrected (26:12-19; cf. Rev. 20:4-6). This time, just as in Rev. 20:10, God brings about the final demise of the great serpent, the dragon Leviathan:[61]

[60] It should be noted that John is not the only New Testament author who reads Isa. 26:10-11 as an oracle of the final judgment and destruction of the unrepentant: so does the author of Hebrews (10:27).

[61] John makes an absolutely unmistakable cross-reference to Isa. 27:1 in Rev. 20:2, referring to Satan as "the dragon, the old serpent." He clearly wants us to understand his visions in 20:1-10 by reference to their parallels in Isaiah 24–27.

Isa. 26:20–27:5

20 Come, my people, enter your chambers,
and shut your doors behind you;
hide yourselves for a little while
until the wrath is past.
21 For the LORD comes out from his place
to punish the inhabitants of the earth for their iniquity;
the earth will disclose the blood shed on it,
and will no longer cover its slain.

27:1 On that day the LORD with his cruel and great and strong sword will punish Leviathan the fleeing serpent, Leviathan the twisting serpent, and he will kill the dragon that is in the sea.

2 On that day:
A pleasant vineyard, sing about it!
3 I, the LORD, am its keeper;
every moment I water it.
I guard it night and day
so that no one can harm it;
4 I have no wrath.
Will someone give me thorns and briars in battle?
I will march against them
and burn them up completely.
5 Instead, let them take hold of my protection.
Let them make peace with me.
Let them make peace with me.[62]

Like Isa. 26:10-11, Isa. 26:20–27:5 imagines a final confrontation between God and the potential attackers of his beloved people. The context of God's glorious kingdom (the description

[62] Verses 4-5 are my own translation. The NRSV rendering of vv. 4-5 (see below) assumes that the vineyard, symbolic of the chosen nation, is the entity against which God threatens to go to battle, which breaches both the immediate context on both sides (vv. 2-3, 5) and the larger preceding context (24:23–27:3):

4 I have no wrath. | If it gives me thorns and briers, | I will march to battle against it. | I will burn it up. | 5 Or else let it cling to me for protection, | let it make peace with me, | let it make peace with me.

of which begins in 24:23) remains unbroken here. In 26:20-21, God gently shepherds his beloved inside so that they do not have to witness the supernatural destruction of those who wish them harm. In 27:2-5, God makes an appeal to those who might be thinking of harming the community of his subjects by using the metaphor of someone trying to introduce harmful, thorny weeds to his precious vineyard. "I bear no hostility towards you," says God. "But try it, and I will completely burn up the thorns." As though to extend a final earnest invitation to reconciliation that contains within it a final warning, God concludes by repeating the words, "Let them make peace with me! Let them make peace with me!"

John's story of the end of Satan and the resurrection and annihilation of "rest of the dead" makes clear and meaningful sense with or without Isaiah 24–27 as a backdrop. But when we accept John's invitation to read these prophecies together, we learn from Isaiah a great deal about God's *reasons* for bringing final destruction upon the "lost." They are utterly and finally destroyed not so much because of what they have done in their mortal lives, but because they prove themselves—even in resurrection—irredeemably wedded to their former hatred and destructiveness. We find in Isaiah yet another oracle in which God ends by making a double appeal for reconciliation and peace:

Isa. 57:15-21

> 15 For thus says the high and lofty one
> who inhabits eternity, whose name is Holy:
> I dwell in the high and holy place,
> and also with those who are contrite and humble in spirit,
> to revive the spirit of the humble,
> and to revive the heart of the contrite.
> 16 For I will not continually accuse,
> nor will I always be angry;
> for then the spirits would grow faint before me,
> even the souls that I have made.
> 17 Because of their wicked covetousness I was angry;
> I struck them, I hid and was angry;
> but they kept turning back to their own ways.

18 I have seen their ways, but I will heal them;
I will lead them and repay them with comfort,
creating for their mourners the fruit of the lips.[63]
Peace, peace, to the far and the near, says the LORD,
and I will heal them.
But the wicked are like the tossing sea
that cannot keep still;
its waters toss up mire and mud.
There is no peace, says my God, for the wicked.

Summary Remarks on Rev. 20:1-10

The brief exposition of Rev. 20:1-10 that I have provided is natural and unforced. At the same time, it befits John's highly sophisticated and densely allusive narrative-building style. The reading that I propose smoothly integrates the passage with all of the prior narrative material in Revelation.[64] It grows directly out of responsiveness to the clues that John continuously provides to the meaning of his own vision narrative—especially his cross-references to texts both in Revelation and in the corpus of OT prophetic literature.[65] On top of all this, it opens up a new and theologically rich way of understanding the purpose for which God brings the unrepentant back to life through resurrection. They are raised to give them a new start—an opportunity to taste, and to join in, the life of the world to come. Just as the first humans turned against God in the first Paradise, bringing mortality, the first death, upon themselves and their progeny in this first creation, so all of the unrepentant are destined to turn against God in the last Paradise, the new creation (Rev. 22:1-3). Their response to the final invitation to join peacefully in the community of God may be foreknown, but the invitation is as real as the life-sustaining fruit offered to Adam and Eve. This time, however, the *second death* (Rev. 2:11; 20:6,

[63] This verse is rather allusive, but "the fruit of the lips" seems to refer to praise to God for his grace (cf. Ps. 51:15; Heb. 13:15).
[64] As we will see below, it will be somewhat more challenging to integrate Rev. 20:1-10 smoothly with what follows.
[65] For a more thorough exegesis of Rev. 20:1-10 and its context, see Mealy, *After the Thousand Years* (see p. 10 nt. 1 above), 95-142; Mealy, *End of the Unrepentant* (see p. 29 nt. 44 above), 122-27, 58-68, 158-83.

14-15; 21:8), the final and irrevocable death, will instantly confront them when, tempted by and with the devil, they eat again of the tree of the knowledge of good and evil (Prov. 26:11; 2 Pet. 2:22).[66]

It is important to be aware, as we set about interpreting the following verses, that they come right after John has finished narrating the final judgment and disposition of all the evil characters in Revelation—the beast, the false prophet, the devil, and all of the unrepentant. The beast and the false prophet have been destroyed by fire (19:20), and the devil and "the rest of the dead" have been tried, sentenced to a long imprisonment, released on probation, and finally destroyed by fire as well (19:21–20:10). On the positive side, the community of the faithful, now freed from all threat from evil, will now presumably go on living and reigning with Christ in the "Beloved City" (20:9) age after age without end. With the story of the "end" thus wrapped up, what remains to be narrated? The apparent answer is *nothing*. It will thus come as no surprise if all the things that John now sees reveal themselves to be new viewpoints on things that he has already seen.

Exposition of Rev. 20:11-15

Rev. 20:11 (my translation)

> $_{11}$And I saw a great white throne, and the One who sat on it—he from whose presence earth and heaven fled away, and no room was found for them.[67]

[66] For more discussion of the theological implications of Rev. 20:1-10, see Mealy, *After the Thousand Years* (see p. 10 nt. 1 above), 234-35, 244-48; Mealy, *End of the Unrepentant* (see p. 29 nt. 44 above), 207-209.

[67] All major English Bible versions mistranslate this verse, erroneously assuming that John intends to narrate the fleeing of earth and heaven from the presence of the Enthroned One. My translation, in agreement with Richmond Lattimore's *The New Testament: A New Translation by Richmond Lattimore* (London: J.M. Dent, 1998), interprets the relative clause "from whose presence..." (Gr. οὗ ἀπὸ τοῦ προσώπου) as a description of the Enthroned One that cross-refers to John's previous visions in 6:14-16 and 16:17-20. Grammatical statistics prove this out. Of the 66 relative clauses in the visionary portion of Revelation (1:9–22:17), not one carries forward the

The Enthroned One, as John's readers know from multiple previous encounters with him in Revelation, is God. It might be tempting to imagine Jesus as well here, since he won the victory and now sits with his Father on his throne (Rev. 3:21; cf. 5:13; 6:16-17; 7:9-10), but the exclusive focus here is on God the Father. John reminds us that he has seen earth and heaven flee from the Enthroned One in his earlier visions:

Rev. 6:14 (cf. 6:16)

> 14 The sky vanished like a scroll rolling itself up,[68] and every mountain and island was removed from its place.

Rev. 16:17-20

> 17 The seventh angel poured his bowl into the air, and a loud voice came out of the temple, from the throne, saying, "It is done!" 18 And there came flashes of lightning, rumblings, peals of thunder, and a violent earthquake, such as had not occurred since people were upon the earth, so violent was that earthquake. 19 The great city was split into three parts, and the cities of the nations fell. God remembered great Babylon and gave her the winecup of the fury of his wrath. 20 And every island fled away, and no mountains were to be found.

These two visions, alluded to in Rev. 20:11, show the elements of the creation fleeing away when confronted with the presence of God on his throne, and they are both associated with the Parousia of God and Jesus. Are we therefore to expect (1) that what John sees in 20:12 is connected to the Parousia, which would make this scene a temporal recapitulation? or (2) that John is about to see something that takes place in the presence of the throne *after* the events of Rev. 20:1-10? Both of these options are equally viable in principle at the threshold of 20:12. All we know so far, at the end of 20:11, is *who* John sees sitting

narrative action. Every one is descriptive. For more detail on this, including my correspondence with Lattimore about the verse, see Mealy, *After the Thousand Years* (see p. 10 nt. 1 above), 164-67.

[68] The image John wants to evoke is that the sky rips and snaps apart like the two ends of a worn-out scroll that curl away from the middle and wrap around their spindles. The blue sky rushes away on both sides from the theophany of "him who sits on the throne" (6:16).

on the throne, not *what is going to happen*. On one hand, John has already had seven revelations of the Parousia,[69] so another vision of Parousia-related happenings would not be any particular surprise. On the other hand, the usual conventions of narrative development lead us, unless we are given clues to the contrary, to assume that whatever John *sees* next *happens* next. Thus we are left, at the end of Rev. 20:11, in a kind of interpretive suspense. What we conclude about the chronological context of what he sees in the scene that now unfolds will depend on what he sees, and how he describes it.

Rev. 20:12

> 12 And I saw the dead, great and small, standing before the throne, and books were opened. Also another book was opened, the book of life. And the dead were judged according to their works, as recorded in the books.

John's description here cross-refers both to Rev. 11:18, which announced that the Parousia would be the moment for "the dead to be judged," and to the Parousia vision of Daniel 7, in which God's throne appeared, hundreds of millions of people stood before him, the court was convened, and "the books were opened" (Dan. 7:9-10). Given these two separate cross-references to the Parousia, we can be confident in understanding that John is seeing here a new vision of the Parousia, *not* what happens after the end of the thousand years.

This scene appears to represent the negative side of the Parousia judgment that John described in mostly positive terms in Rev. 20:4-6. This time, rather than seeing the court decree the *reward* of resurrection for those faithful witnesses whose "lives" (or *souls*, Gr. ψυχή) have been sheltered by God in heaven (cf. 6:9-11; 12:10-12; 14:13; 20:4), we see the *judgment* of "the dead" according to their works in mortal life as recorded in the books. What is the outcome for these "dead," who are judged according to the things they did in mortal life? To find this out, we have to read on to verse 13:

[69] See Rev. 6:12-17; 7:9-17; 11:15-19; 14:14-20; 16:17-21; 19:5-9 (audition); 19:11-21; 20:4-6.

Rev. 20:13-15

> 13 And the sea gave up the dead that were in it, Death and Hades gave up the dead that were in them, and all were judged according to what they had done. 14 Then Death and Hades were thrown into the lake of fire. This is the second death, the lake of fire; 15 and anyone whose name was not found written in the book of life was thrown into the lake of fire.

The outcome of the judgment of v. 12 is that the dead are drawn out of the realms of the dead and—in the state of resurrection—are judged according to their actions (v. 13). This is the same two-stage judgment sequence that we just witnessed! In 20:5, the court found "the rest of the dead" unworthy of resurrection at Christ's coming; it was decreed that they be raised "when the thousand years were completed." Then, after the thousand years, they were resurrected and judged according to their post-resurrection actions, which earned them the penalty of fiery destruction (Rev. 20:8-9). Rev. 20:14-15, in slightly different symbols (a pool of fire that drowns them, rather than a deluge of fire from heaven that consumes them),[70] pictures the identical ultimate fate. A number of clues confirm that this is what John intends us to understand.

1. Rev. 2:11 and 20:6 make it clear that those who are faithful to Jesus will not be vulnerable to the "second death," which we now (upon reading 20:14) understand to be the meaning of the picture of "the lake (pool) of fire." Death and total incineration both describe the final destruction of the unrepentant. Twice granted the gift of bodily life, the unrepentant twice misuse it. The *second* death, unlike the first, is irrevocable.

2. Rev. 20:15 makes a direct correlation between those whose names are not written in the Book of Life, on the one hand, and those thrown into the pool of fire, on the other hand. John later

[70] LSJ defines λίμνη as "a pool of water left by the sea or a river." It is easy enough to picture the "river of fire" that comes from the throne of God in Dan. 7:9-11 going forth to inundate and incinerate the fourth beast (cf. Rev. 19:20). It is equally easy to imagine that the deluge of fiery destruction that comes down from heaven upon the resurrected unrepentant in Rev. 20:9 gathers into a great pool that incinerates not only them but the devil (20:10).

clarifies that the Book of Life is the book of the citizen-rolls of the New Jerusalem, the people of God (21:27; 22:14, 18), also known as the Beloved City (20:9). Those resurrected *outside* the city are judged by their actions and are destroyed by fire (Isa. 26:10-11 || Rev. 20:8-9 || 20:13-15). In Revelation, one of whose most striking features is its multiple complementary representations of the same realities, this is not a coincidence.[71]

3. The "great white throne," not encountered before in Revelation, is not exactly "white," but rather *shining*, or *bright*.[72] This points us to John's description of the New Jerusalem in Rev. 21:9-11, which "…has the glory of God.[73] The source of her light[74] was like a priceless gem, like a crystal-clear diamond."[75] The New Jerusalem, the Bride, the Beloved City—which we have briefly seen in Rev. 20:9—*is itself God's great, glorious throne* (cf. Jer. 3:14-17; 17:12-13; *1 Enoch* 18:6-9; 24:1–25:5). In retrospect, it becomes clear that being resurrected, surrounding the "Beloved City" in order to attack it, and being destroyed by fire (20:8-9) is exactly the same experience as being resurrected in front of God's "great, shining throne," being judged

[71] The Parousia in particular is represented multiple times (see the eight refs in nt. 69 on p. 40, and add 20:11-12; 21:1-8), but a number of other eschatological events are also represented twice or more, e.g. the resurrection and exaltation of Jesus (5:1-14; 12:1-5), the coming of the New Jerusalem (21:1-2; 21:9–22:5), the downfall of Babylon the Great (17:16-18; 18:16-19; 18:21), and the (pseudo-)resurrection of the beast (13:1; 13:3, 14; 17:1-8).
[72] LSJ first definition for λευκός is "light, bright, clear."
[73] See Isa. 60:1, 2, 19.
[74] Gr. ὁ φωστὴρ αὐτῆς, i.e. God, whose glory illuminates the New Jerusalem. Modern English translations of Rev. 21:11 variously mistranslate the Greek word φωστήρ as "light" (NKJV, ISV, WEB) or "brilliance" (NIV, NASB, NET) or "radiance" (NRSV, ESV, HCSB), as though John were referring to the light that *she* emits. To the contrary, the word φωστήρ refers to a source of light that shines *on* something, not the light that shines *from* something. And God, who illuminates her (Rev. 21:23; 22:5), has already been compared to a shining jasper in Rev. 4:3.
[75] Lit. "like an exceedingly costly gemstone of crystal-clear jasper" (i.e. quartz). Diamond was known to the ancients as an exceedingly hard substance, but they knew nothing of the clear gemstone that throws off glints of brilliant color. Because diamond is the most precious clear gemstone familiar to moderns, I have used this culturally appropriate translation.

on the basis of your actions, and being destroyed by fire (20:11, 13-15).

4. John has already shown us that the same judgment event can be pictured first as a battle (Rev. 19:11-21), then as a courtroom scene (Rev. 20:4-6).[76] The very same pattern—with focus on the judgment of the unrepentant—repeats itself in 20:7-10 and 20:11-15. This too is no coincidence.

This fourth point opens the door to some significant theological wisdom. Human beings are not simply created as individual units. They are also designed to live and function together as members of a larger corporate entity. In an important sense, each person individually corresponds to humanity as a whole as the individual cells of the human body correspond to the body as a whole. Of course, Jesus and Paul both picture the faithful as members of a living body whose chief member is Jesus himself.[77] This corporate entity partakes of a meaningful existence and identity unto itself, both spiritually and ethically: the whole is greater than the sum of the parts. This implies that human beings are beloved by God and accountable to God not just as individuals, but also as corporate groups—on all levels, right up to faithful humanity as a whole ("the Bride") and unrepentant humanity as a whole ("Gog and Magog"). John's vision in Rev. 20:7-10, together with Isaiah's visions in Isa. 26:10-11; 26:21–27:5, reveals the last act in God's judgment of unrepentant *corporate* humanity. Complementary to this, John's vision of Rev. 20:13-15 reveals the last act in God's judgment with focus on the unrepentant as *individuals*. The wording of Rev. 20:13 makes this explicit: "they were *each* judged on the basis of their actions." The two visions represent the same judgment, considered from two equally important, and equally indispensable, perspectives.

[76] Rev. 11:18, in announcing the Parousia, highlights both the battle and the trial themes.

[77] Jn 15:1-5; Rom. 12:5; 1 Cor. 10:17; 12:12-27; Eph. 1:22-23; 2:14-22; 4:15-16, 25; 5:30; Col. 1:18, 24; 2:19.

Two Complications That Open Out to Further Theological Insights

First Complication: What is to be made of the fact that the thousand-year gap between the Parousia judgment and the final judgment of the unrepentant (seen in Rev. 20:5-10) is not mentioned between Rev. 20:12 and Rev. 20:13?

There are two ways to account for this noticeable absence. The first way relates to the observation made under clue 4 above. The similarities and differences between 20:4-10 and 20:11-15 point to the presence of two complementary perspectives: focus on corporate judgment, and focus on individual judgment. Rev. 20:4 and 20:12 share the following *similarities*:

- John in both places sees a courtroom scene that he understands to be the Parousia judgment scene described in Daniel 7.
- In each case he also sees the outcome—resurrection to life and reigning with Christ for the "souls" (Gr. αἱ ψυχαί) of the faithful in 20:4, and resurrection to a final negative judgment according to actions for the "dead" (οἱ νεκροί) in 20:13.
- In each case he sees those who do not belong to the people of God judged according to their actions and destroyed by fire (20:9, 14-15).

There are also three major *differences* between the two visions:

- In 20:12-15 the courtroom setting persists throughout.
- In 20:12-15 there is no mention of the deceptive role and final fate of Satan.
- In 20:12-15 there is no mention of a temporal gap between the judgment of the dead according to their past actions ("the things written in the books," v. 12), on the one hand, and their judgment as resurrected people according to their actions in their new, resurrected condition, on the other hand (v. 13).

These three elements of difference are all traceable to the fact that 20:11-15 focuses exclusively on individual accountability and judgment, rather than on the eschatological story-line of the last (corporate) judgment of the massed foes of God and his people. In Isaiah 24–27, Ezekiel 38, and Rev. 20:1-3, 7-10, we read a story of "the end" in which the people of God corporately enjoy the peace of God's kingdom for a long time, after which their old enemies are brought on the scene and destroyed before they can violently attack the community of the faithful. The individual and transcendental perspective of Rev. 20:11-15 *complements*, and *does not overwrite*, this corporate and narrative perspective on "the end."

A second and equally pertinent way to explain the fact that the thousand-year delay is not mentioned is to observe that this scene (20:11-15) is composed so as to distill the entire double judgment of 20:4-10 into one great courtroom scene. Consequently, all temporal elements are simply abstracted out.[78] Thus, despite the fact that the previously-revealed bifurcation of God's judgment of unrepentant human beings lies right on the surface of Rev. 20:12-13,[79] Rev. 20:11-15 as a whole leaves the impression of being one great trial or judgment scene. Rev. 20:11-15 presents the entire process of judgment of human beings—encompassing everything they do in their mortal *and* resurrected lives—as one total divine assessment. This leads to a theological insight: from the perspective of God, the Alpha and the Omega, the entire temporal existence of each created being is visible at once. Before the Eternal and Omniscient One, human beings stand accountable for the totality of the existence they have been given. As above, the a-temporal and transcendental perspective of Rev. 20:11-15 does not *replace*, but rather

[78] The scene is not specifically placed in time (as noted above), nor is there mention of the thousand years, nor is the unending nature of the pool of fire (see 20:10) mentioned here. This scene focuses on the *what* of divine judgment, not on the *when* or the *how long*.

[79] That is, God *judges the dead*, for deeds done in mortal life, 20:4-5 || 20:12; then God *raises and judges them in a state of resurrection*, for deeds done in a state of resurrection, 20:8-9 || 20:13. Revelation commentators who do not understand that Rev. 20:7-10 narrates the resurrection and judgment of the unrepentant often remark on the oddity of Rev. 20:13 following upon Rev. 20:12. R.H. Charles, for example, simply states, "This verse [20:13] should be transferred before 12" (*The Revelation of St. John*, II [ICC; Edinburgh: T. & T. Clark, 1920], 194). Commentators inclined to respect the integrity of the text typically note the oddity, but choose to read v. 13 as an elaborating restatement of v. 12.

complements, the traditional prophetic and history-like perspective of Rev. 20:1-10.

Second Complication: What is to be made of the fact that on this reading we appear to end up with two differing pictures of final punishment—instant annihilation by fire (Rev. 20:9), and everlasting torment (19:20; 20:10, 14-15, cf. 14:9-11)? Are these two pictures, like the final battle and final trial images, ultimately to be understood as complementary perspectives on the same reality? If so, what does each tell us?

In the first place, the annihilation image of Rev. 20:9 traces deep OT roots to the instant destruction of Sodom and Gomorrah by fire and sulfur from heaven (Gen. 19:24-25, 27-28). Three separate OT prophecies (Deut. 29:23; Jer. 49:18; 50:39-40; Zeph. 2:9) locate the significance of this event in the fact that the destruction is *permanent*—the burning leaves behind it a salt waste that can never again support habitation. This is an important point of background to Revelation 20, because the resurgence of the devil and the unrepentant in 20:7-8 (after their dramatic removal from the earth in 19:17–20:2) raises the uncomfortable question: if these dangerous enemies have been raised once, what assurance do we have that God will not allow them to come back yet again at some future point to menace the faithful? The image in Rev. 20:9 of a consuming fire from heaven, thanks to its resonance with Gen. 19:24-25 and its daughter passages, speaks directly to that insecurity. It says, this is the *final* end of these enemies. There will be no further attack. Added to this, the image of a "lake/pool of fire," which never releases those consigned to it, offers the same assurance in a different and equally pointed way. We are told in no uncertain terms that Satan, the beast, the false prophet, and all of "the rest of the dead" will never escape from this second, and final, death (cf. Rev. 20:10, implying the same fate for those cast into it in 20:14-15).

It is clear that this pair of images functions to double-underline the finality of the destruction of the devil and the unrepentant. But beyond this, would John want for us to think more literalistically about the lake/pool of fire—imagining, for example, that the fire that flows down from heaven (20:9) pools to form a permanent lake (20:10, 14-15)? Is the "everlastingness" of the torment of the lake/pool of fire thus to be understood literally? I think not, for two reasons additional to the facts that (1) the lake/pool of fire is made to refer to the same fate as the annihilating fire from heaven, and (2) the lake/pool of fire is interpreted as "the second death."

Thirdly, since the enemies of 20:8-9 had "surrounded" the Beloved City, and all of them were consumed by fire from heaven, the more literalistic approach would result in the exceedingly ugly idea that the inhabitants of the New Jerusalem will find themselves surrounded on all sides by numberless hordes in fiery torment for all eternity. It is arbitrary to resist taking this image literally in three dimensions, but then insist on taking it literally in the fourth dimension.

Fourthly, John introduces and develops the whole concept of everlasting torment by means of multiple cross-references to the oracle against Edom in Isaiah 34, which you can examine in the comparison table on the following page.

Two things are to be noted from these unmistakable verbal connections—fire/burning, sulfur, smoke, night and day/day and night, forever and ever. First, Isaiah's oracle clearly employs the language of never-ending burning in order to emphasize the *completeness* and *permanence* of the destruction being prophesied (see again Deut. 29:23; Jer. 49:18; 50:39-40; Zeph. 2:9). No one can ever rebuild ruins that never cool down; no one can ever grow crops in sulfur-poisoned soil; no one can survive at all in a land whose streams run with molten, burning tar, not water. Isaiah's oracle employs both physical and temporal hyperboles here, in order to assure God's people that their perennial enemy, Edom, *will never, ever be a threat again.* Isaiah does not intend, nor would any but the crassest and most narrow-minded literalist understand, that we should take the picture of forever-burning tar streams literally.[80] What is more, John is an extremely astute reader of Isaiah, and his detailed

[80] Christian interpreters, who embrace the promise of a new heavens and a new earth that comes later in Isaiah (65:17-25; 66:22), would have to posit the grotesque idea that God will miraculously lift the smoking hulk of Edom (and Babylon the Great, Rev. 19:3) from the earth while dissolving and renewing the whole cosmos, and then set them down in the new creation so that they can spew their toxic smoke into the skies of the new creation forever.

cross-references signal that he is intentionally using same device of temporal hyperbole.[81] The theological punch line: the problematical doctrine of a hell of everlasting torment cannot be founded on these verses when they are correctly interpreted within their larger prophetic context.[82]

Isa. 34:9-10	Rev. 14:9-11	Rev. 18:8; 19:3	Rev. 20:10
9 … And the streams of Edom[83] shall be turned into pitch, and her soil into ***sulfur***; her land shall become **burning** pitch.	9 "If someone worships the beast and his image 10 …They're going to be tormented with **fire** and ***sulfur***…	8 she will be burned up with **fire**	10 And the devil, who was deceiving them, was thrown into the lake of **fire** and ***sulfur***—where both the beast and the false prophet are.
10 **Night and day** it shall not be quenched; its ***smoke*** shall ***go up*** **forever.** From generation to generation it shall lie waste; no one shall pass through it **forever and ever**.	11 The ***smoke*** from their torment ***goes up*** **forever and ever.** And those who worship the beast and his image get no rest **day and night**…	3 Her ***smoke goes up*** **forever and ever!**	They're going to be tormented **day and night, forever and ever.**

[81] For more in-depth comments on the relationship between Rev. 14:9-11; 18:8; 19:3; 20:10 and Isa. 34:10-11, see Mealy, *End of the Unrepentant* (see p. 29 nt. 44 above), 80-83, 85-86.

[82] Nor is it necessary—or consistent with the witness of the vast majority of Scripture—to infer this doctrine from a small handful of other passages in the New Testament. For a thorough exegetical study of all biblical passages from Genesis to Revelation that describe or predict fire and/or being consumed for the unrepentant, see Mealy, *End of the Unrepentant* (see p. 29 nt. 44 above). Similarly, but broader in scope, see E. Fudge, *The Fire That Consumes: A Biblical and Historical Study of the Doctrine of Final Punishment* (3rd edn; Eugene, OR: Wipf & Stock, 2011).

[83] Hebrew *her streams* [cf. Isa. 34:5, 6].

Summary Remarks on Rev. 20:7-15

Historic premillennialists have often tried hard to resist evidences of recapitulation in Revelation in general, in order specifically to resist an amillennial reading of Rev. 20:1-10. Recapitulation, however, functions as one of the central literary devices in Revelation. Moreover, John trains his readers progressively, as his vision narrative unfolds, to recognize when recapitulation is happening. Careful cross-references to texts within Revelation and within the corpus of biblical prophecy guide the readers in identifying instances when John understands himself to be seeing a new viewpoint on something that he—or another prophet—has seen before. John, an avid reader and student of OT prophecy, well knows that the Spirit inspires multiple visions or prophecies of the same realities.

In following through a new and independent exposition of Rev. 19:5–20:15,[84] I have demonstrated a reading that is responsive to the connected flow of the text as it unfolds. It also meaningfully relates each portion to the co-texts to which John frequently points us by use of cross-references. This reading encounters some complications of its own—but they arise from and derive coherent positive meaning from the very cross-references that John uses all the time in Revelation. As a bonus, it gives rise to three theological insights that offer enrichment to our understanding of Revelation and biblical eschatology:

1. Human beings are created to take part in both an individual and a corporate identity, and they are thus accountable to their Creator on both of these levels.
2. The scope of God's ultimate judgment of human beings takes in their entire existence, including their existence as resurrected persons.
3. The theologically problematical concept of everlasting torment for the unrepentant finds itself without

[84] This exposition does not pretend to be a thorough commentary on the text. Its aim, instead, is to present a concise demonstration of a way in which the text may reasonably be interpreted. I have intentionally spent little time on the many exegetical decisions that could have been answered one way or the other without affecting the overall cogency of the reading being developed, and I have only hit the highlights of the arguments in favor of this reading.

> exegetical underpinning in Revelation when we realize that Rev. 20:7-10 and Rev. 20:13-15 present two viewpoints on one final trial resulting in one final sentence: "the second death."

A Millennial Reign in Heaven above a Lifeless Earth?

I'd like to finish out this exposition by spending a moment in dialogue with the Seventh Day Adventist view of the millennium. The mainstream Seventh Day Adventist view, since founding generation biblical expositor Uriah Smith brought it forward in his *Commentary on Daniel and the Revelation*,[85] has always been that the thousand-year reign of the saints takes place in heaven, in a New Jerusalem that hovers above the formless and desolate earth. This model, by correctly understanding that the battle of Rev. 20:7-10 refers to the resurrection of the unrepentant, escapes many of the serious drawbacks of historic premillennialism and amillennialism. It nonetheless suffers from its own major weaknesses. First, it interposes, without substantial evidence in Revelation itself, a thousand-year gap between the Parousia, with its radical dissolution of the cosmos, and the new creation.[86] Secondly, it situates the promised reign of the saints in heaven for an entire age, leaving them with nothing to reign over. On this reading, the earth (the context for humanity's original dominion over all living things in Genesis 1) remains completely lifeless for the millennial age. Thirdly, on this view the scene of Rev. 20:7-10 ends up making no sense, because the resurrected unrepentant are left without the slightest ability either to "surround" or to fight a "battle" with the New Jerusalem in Rev. 20:8. They are resurrected onto the earth, and the New Jerusalem is imagined to be hovering in heaven, there awaiting the dissolution and re-creation of the heavens and earth. To the contrary, the language of Rev. 20:8-9 clearly implies that the siege of "the camp of the saints, the Beloved City" takes place "on the broad plain of the earth" *because that is where the Beloved City stands.* This earthly context is confirmed when we look at the key prophetic co-texts

[85] Hagerstown, MD: Review and Herald Publishing, 2006 (1881).

[86] On the fact that the dissolution and the re-creation of the cosmos belong together, see the exposition of Rev. 21:1-8 below.

to which John points us (Isa. 24–27; Ezek. 36–38), and when we correctly understand that Rev. 21:1–22:5 recapitulates the Parousia. Accordingly, we now turn to the final section of our exposition, Rev. 21:1-8.

Exposition of Rev. 21:1-8

Rev. 21:1

> 1 Then I saw a new heaven and a new earth; for the first heaven and the first earth had passed away, and the sea was no more.

John speaks here not of a new *and different* (Gr. νέος) heaven and earth, but of a *renewed* (Gr. καινός) heaven and earth. John had earlier seen the first heaven and earth dissolve and lose their form (Rev. 6:14; 11:19; 20:11). The earth, like Jesus her Architect and Savior, and like his faithful witnesses, had suffered violence, and ultimately murder, at the hand of humanity (Rev. 11:18; Isa. 24:5, 18-20). But earth and heaven have now been *resurrected*, just as in Paul's vision of the future of the cosmos in Rom. 8:18-23 (quoted on p. 90 below).[87]

In John's description of his vision of the resurrected cosmos, he says (translating literally) that "the sea isn't there anymore, and the Holy City, the New Jerusalem, I saw coming down out of heaven from God." Because of this immediate association between the absence of "the sea" and John's vision of the New Jerusalem coming down from above, it appears that John may be referring to the glassy sea, the glassy/icy dome that in this age is imagined to form an opaque ceiling to the earthly realm and a transparent floor to heaven, God's heavenly temple and throne room (see 4:1-6; 15:2).[88] The barrier that has separated God's habitation from ours is removed, and so God, together with all the holy ones (faithful angels and human beings), now

[87] Admittedly, the theme of birth-giving, which for Paul links the rebirth of the cosmos and our rebirth in resurrection, is not present here in Rev. 21:1—although this idea of resurrection as a kind of birth-giving traces OT roots to Isa. 26:17-19.
[88] John pictures something analogous to one-way glass. From heaven, God can see everything in the human realm, but human beings can see nothing of God and God's realm (Exod. 24:9-11 is the exception that proves the rule).

comes down to dwell on the renewed earth. From now on, "the earth will be filled with the knowledge of (the glory of) God as the waters cover the sea" (Isa. 11:9; Hab. 2:14; cf. Rev. 21:10-11; 22:5). From now on, human beings will (metaphorically) see God face to face (22:4; cf. 1 Cor. 13:12). The following verse (Rev. 21:3) is going to express this new condition in its own way.

It may also be that John sees no sea in the newly resurrected cosmos because in biblical cosmology, the sea retains a certain element of wildness and chaos, as though God, in creating this world, has left a portion of the present cosmos in its "unformed" and untamed state:

Job 38:4-11

> 4 "Where were you when I laid the foundation of the earth?
> Tell me, if you have understanding.
> 5 Who determined its measurements—surely you know!
> Or who stretched the line upon it?
> 6 On what were its bases sunk,
> or who laid its cornerstone
> 7 when the morning stars sang together
> and all the heavenly beings[89] shouted for joy?
> 8 "Or who shut in the sea with doors
> when it burst out from the womb?—
> 9 when I made the clouds its garment,
> and thick darkness its swaddling band,
> 10 and prescribed bounds for it,
> and set bars and doors,
> 11 and said, 'Thus far shall you come, and no farther,
> and here shall your proud waves be stopped'?"

Ps. 89:9-11

> 9 You rule the raging of the sea;
> when its waves rise, you still them.
> 10 You crushed Rahab[90] like a carcass;

[89] Lit. *sons of God.*

[90] Rahab is a mythological sea monster which here symbolizes the wildness and untamable character of the sea.

you scattered your enemies with your mighty arm.
11 The heavens are yours, the earth also is yours;
the world and all that is in it—you have founded them.

Jer. 5:22

22 Do you not fear me? says the LORD;
Do you not tremble before me?
I placed the sand as a boundary for the sea,
a perpetual barrier that it cannot pass;
though the waves toss, they cannot prevail,
though they roar, they cannot pass over it.

Perhaps in the cosmology of John's new creation vision, the sea is not visible at the beginning because no portion of the resurrected cosmos is left wild and unformed. If any sea is eventually to exist in the new creation, it must therefore come into being gradually, continuously fed by the River of Life.[91]

Rev. 21:2

> 2 And I saw the holy city, the new Jerusalem, coming down out of heaven from God, prepared as a bride adorned for her husband.

John's description of the New Jerusalem as "prepared as a bride adorned for her husband" unmistakably takes us back to the wedding theme, which had been put on pause during the presentation of a series of four judgment scenes (Rev. 19:11–20:3; 20:4-6; 20:7-10; 20:11-15).[92] Cross-references to Rev. 19:7-8 come in the form of the shared description of the Bride as "prepared" (Gr. ἡτοιμάζω), in the symmetry between "his bride" in 19:7 and "her husband" in 21:2, and in the reference in each passage to the special beauty of the bride on her wedding day. Similarly, in 19:8 John writes that the fine linen fabric of the Bride's wedding gown represents the "righteous deeds of

[91] A related concept is found in vision of Ezek. 47:1-12, where a spring from beneath the foundation of the Temple becomes a great river that converts the sea to fresh water. John calls this river the River of the Water of Life (Rev. 22:1-2). For the idea that rivers are the source for the water of the sea, see Eccl. 1:7.

[92] Note the alternation of focus: corporate, individual, corporate, individual.

the saints," and this points forward to the appearance of the New Jerusalem, the Bride, who represents the corporate community of the saints (i.e. the holy ones). The theme of the mystery of corporate and individual identity is at play here again in relation to this positive vision of the Bride, just as it was in the previous negative scenes: 19:17-21 and 20:4-6, 20:7-10 and 20:11-15.

Given that the dissolution and the re-creation of the cosmos logically go together, and that the wedding of the Lamb and the Bride is obviously a metaphor for the Parousia, we need harbor no significant doubt that John is here seeing a vision of the Parousia that complements his audition that announced the Parousia in 19:5-9.[93] The renewed "voice from the throne" that now follows (Rev. 21:3 || 19:5) also helps us tie the two passages together:

Rev. 21:3-4

3 And I heard a loud voice from the throne saying,

> "See, the home[94] of God is among mortals.[95]
> He will dwell with them;
> they will be his people[s],[96]
> and God himself will be with them;[97]
> 4 he will wipe every tear from their eyes.[98]

[93] For more detailed and wide-ranging arguments that Rev. 21:1-2 is to be understood as a vision of the Parousia, see pp. 77-83 below.
[94] Lit. "tent"; this is the presence of God on earth that was hinted at and hoped for in the divinely revealed symbols of the Tent of Meeting/Witness (e.g. Exod. 25–30 and 40:34-38) and the Temple (e.g. 1 Kgs 5–8; 2 Chron. 6:18; 7:1-3). For the promise of God's final dwelling with humanity, see Ezek. 37:27.
[95] Lit. "with human beings."
[96] NRSV, following the earliest ancient mss, has "peoples" here, rather than "people." The reading "people" seems so proper and correct (see the OT quotations below, esp. Zech. 2:11) that it's equally hard to imagine (1) John writing "peoples" in the first place, or (2) a copyist consciously replacing "people" with "peoples," thinking that "people" is a mistake. It is, however, relatively easy to imagine that a sleepy copyist who was relatively unfamiliar with the OT might automatically make "peoples" agree in number with the plural subject and verb, "they will be."
[97] Some mss have "And God himself, their God, will be with them."
[98] Isa. 25:8.

> Death will be no more;
> mourning and crying and pain will be no more,[99]
> for the first things have passed away."[100]

The central work of Jesus as Messiah is to reunite estranged humanity with God. God himself now announces that this work has been successfully accomplished. From now on, there will no longer be any separation between God and his people. The Parousia of Christ, his final and complete coming to his people, is thus—as always in Revelation—equally and at the same time the Parousia of God, God's final and complete coming to his people. Rev. 21:3 literally says, "God's tent is with human beings, and he is going to live in a tent with them…" This promise "from the throne" of intimate divine presence and communion in tent imagery (Gr. σκηνή, σκηνόω) underlines the angel's explanation of John's Parousia vision in Rev. 7:9-17:

> 14 Then he said to me, "These are they who have come out of the great ordeal;[101] they have washed their robes and made them white in the blood of the Lamb.
>
> 15 For this reason they are before the throne of God,
> and worship him day and night within his temple,
> and the one who is seated on the throne will shelter them.[102]
> 16 They will hunger no more, and thirst no more;
> the sun will not strike them,
> nor any scorching heat;
> 17 for the Lamb at the center of the throne will be their shepherd,
> and he will guide them to springs of the water of life,
> and God will wipe away every tear from their eyes."

Both Rev. 7:15 and 21:3 cross-refer to the promise God makes to the faithful Israelites in Lev. 26:11-12 (my translation):

[99] Isa. 35:10; 65:17-19.
[100] Isa. 35:10; 43:18; 65:19.
[101] Or "persecution."
[102] Lit. "put up his tent over them" (Gk. σκηνόω).

> 11 I will pitch my tent among you, and will not despise you. 12 I will walk among you and be your God, and you will be my people.

This promise is also carried forward and associated with the coming of Messiah in Ezek. 37:27:

> 27 My dwelling place shall be with them; and I will be their God, and they shall be my people.

The same promise is directed specifically to "the daughter of Zion," symbolic of Jerusalem, in Zech. 2:10-11:

> 10 Sing and rejoice, O daughter Zion! For lo, I will come and dwell[103] in your midst, says the LORD. 11 Many nations shall join themselves to the LORD on that day, and shall be my people; and I will dwell in your midst. And you shall know that the LORD of hosts has sent me to you.

If it weren't already completely obvious that Rev. 21:3-4 is to be understood as a promise of the Parousia of God, which is at the same time the Parousia of Jesus Christ, there are, among the many cross-references in this dense passage, two or possibly even three references to the oracle of the Parousia of God in Isa. 24:23–25:12. We have already seen above (in the comments on Rev. 19:17–20:9) that John looks upon this Isaiah oracle as a revelation of the Parousia.

Isa. 25:7-8

> 7 And he [the LORD] will destroy on this mountain
> the shroud that is cast over all peoples,
> the sheet that is spread over all nations;
> 8 he will swallow up death forever.
> Then the Lord GOD will wipe away the tears from all faces,
> and the disgrace of his people he will take away from all the earth,
> for the LORD has spoken.

[103] Lit. "live in a tent" (Heb. שכן).

The cross-references in Rev. 21:4 to the end of death and the wiping away of all tears are unmistakable, but it is also distinctly possible that John would also want us to understand the "sea of glass" (Rev. 4:6; 15:2) as the "veil that is spread over all nations," separating the dwelling-place of God from that of humanity.[104] Now, in the new creation, the veil is gone. It no longer separates God from his people, and it no longer separates heaven from earth.

Rev. 21:5-6a

> 5 And the one who was seated on the throne said, "See, I am making all things new." Also he said, "Write this, for these words are trustworthy and true." 6 Then he said to me, "It is done![105] I am the Alpha and the Omega,[106] the beginning and the end.

Following on the announcement that God is now fully present with humanity, the Enthroned One explicitly speaks for the first (and only) time in Revelation. God speaks in the first person, and even speaks directly to John. The statements that God makes appear virtually transcendent and timeless. The words "I am making all things new," for example, don't neatly fit with any particular context in time. In John's time they somehow seem too early, and in the context of the new creation they seem too late. Likewise, it would seem insipid to compare the words "They are done" (Rev. 21:6) with the earlier words "It is done," which John heard after the pouring out of the seventh bowl (Rev. 16:17), and simply say that the former indicates the completion of the negative work of judging sinful humanity and wrapping up the first creation, whereas the latter indicates the completion of both that work and the positive work of saving the faithful and bringing in the new creation. No, something deeper is being affirmed: namely, that God is the One who eternally owns the power of creation and re-creation. The process of bringing newness belongs to God and is eternally at work

[104] It might be tempting to interpret death as the veil in Isa. 25:7, since death is mentioned immediately afterwards, but it is hard to see how a veil or covering makes an appropriate metaphor for death.
[105] Lit. "They are done!"
[106] These are the first and last letters of the Greek alphabet.

both in and beyond time as we know it. God is the Alpha and the Omega, the Beginning and the End, the Creator who makes, and sees, and comprehends, and unfolds, everything that was, is, and shall be. From God's perspective, all things are finished before they are even brought into being. Thus God does not just *see* the future; God has in some sense already *created* the future. In God's world, the new heaven and the new earth are already real. God's transcendence of time as Creator explains how God can reveal to prophets such as Isaiah and John things that have not yet happened, and which no human being could ever have imagined:

Isa. 42:9; 43:19; 48:6

> 9 See, the former things have come to pass,
> and new things I now declare;
> before they spring forth,
> I tell you of them.
> 19 I am about to do a new thing;
> now it springs forth, do you not perceive it?
> 6 I will make a way in the wilderness
> and rivers in the desert.
>
> From this time forward I make you hear new things,
> hidden things that you have not known.

Rev. 21:6b-7

> 6 …To the thirsty I will give water as a gift from the spring of the water of life.[107] 7 Those who conquer will inherit these things, and I will be their God and they will be my children.[108]

God promises the victors unlimited access to the spring of the water of life, and this promise refers to the restoration of the relationship that God has intended to have with human beings from the very beginning. God's desire and design for us is that we should depend on God as our continuously flowing artesian well of life (v. 6b):

[107] Isa. 55:1; Jer. 2:13; Ps. 36:9; see Jn 7:37.
[108] See 2 Sam. 7:14, now extended to all the faithful.

Jer. 2:12-13

> 12 Be appalled, O heavens, at this,
> be shocked, be utterly desolate,
> says the LORD,
> 13 for my people have committed two evils:
> they have forsaken me, the fountain of living water,
> and dug out cisterns for themselves,
> cracked cisterns that can hold no water.

Isa. 55:1

> 1 Ho, everyone who thirsts, come to the waters!

It was in order to reconnect us to this source that God sent Jesus to us, as Jesus says in Jn 7:37-38:

> 37 On the last day of the festival, the great day, while Jesus was standing there, he cried out, "Let anyone who is thirsty come to me,[109] 38 and let the one who believes in me drink. As the scripture has said, 'Out of the believer's heart[110] shall flow rivers of living water.'"

Rev. 21:7 also promises the restoration of a fundamental relationship between human beings and God. The promise of child status in relation to God signals the restoration of the familial relationship and identity into which God originally created human beings:

Gen. 1:26-27; 5:1-3 (my translation)

> 26 Let us make humankind in our image, and according to our likeness… 27 So God created humankind in his image, in the image of God…male and female he created them.

> 1 When God created humankind, he made them in the likeness of God. Male and female he created them, and… 3 when Adam had lived 130 years, he became the father of a son in his likeness, according to his image, and named him Seth.

[109] Some good mss lack the words, "to me." Jesus is clearly echoing Isaiah's prophecy (Isa. 55:1), whether the words "to me" are original or not.
[110] Lit. "belly."

Few passages in Scripture unambiguously teach that human beings were created into the identity of children in relation to God, but this pair from Genesis does so in a way that ought to be impossible to miss. Paul, in his public preaching, also boldly affirms this: "For we too are his offspring" (Acts 17:28).[111]

Again, Jesus comes to model and to restore people to this fundamental and original relationship with God: "Pray then in this way: Our Father…" (Mt. 6:9).

Jn 1:12-13

> 12 But to all who received him, who believed in his name, he gave power to become children of God, 13 who were born, not of blood or of the will of the flesh or of the will of man, but of God.

Rev. 21:8

> 8 But as for the cowardly, the faithless,[112] the polluted,[113] the murderers, the fornicators, the sorcerers, the idolaters, and all liars, their place will be in the lake that burns with fire and sulfur, which is the second death.

God finishes the speech that began in Rev. 21:3 with a word of warning. These good things are not for those who value their mortal lives in this age more than the everlasting life that Jesus purchased for them. Such people are *cowards*, who give in to the demands of the beast and the false prophet—or to any lesser form of pressure in this evil age—in order to be spared persecution and martyrdom as witnesses for Jesus. They are *faithless*, because they do not trust God enough to put their mortal lives at risk in the hope of eternal life. As Jesus says,

[111] This is a quotation from a poem by the Stoic philosopher Aratus (*Phaenomena* 5).

[112] Or "the faithless," or "the unbelievers." In John's world, all these amount to the same thing. Those who don't trust God and Christ will eventually prove themselves unwilling to risk their lives for the hope of resurrection, and so they will prove themselves untrustworthy by abandoning their faith under persecution and worshiping the beast.

[113] Lit. "vile." By implication, they're filthy and disgusting because of practices related to idolatry.

Mt. 10:38

> 38 Whoever does not take up their cross[114] and follow me is not worthy of me. 39 Those who find their life will lose it, and those who lose their life for my sake will find it.

Jn 12:24-26

> 24 Very truly, I tell you, unless a grain of wheat falls into the earth and dies, it remains just a single grain; but if it dies, it bears much fruit. 25 Those who love their life lose it, and those who hate their life in this world will keep it for eternal life. 26 Whoever serves me must follow me, and where I am, there will my servant be also. Whoever serves me, the Father will honor.

People who deny their Lord under the threat of persecution end up becoming accessories in the *murder* of their friends in order to save their own necks. They are *liars*, because they deny the Savior who died for them. They are *idolaters*, because they give in to the worship of the beast—and Satan behind him. They will join all the other cowards, unfaithful and faithless people, liars, murderers, sorcerers, and idolaters. They will join those who turned away from the right path not under the pressure of persecution, but simply under the lure of this world's crude and *polluted* pleasures and *sexual immorality*. The Enthroned One warns Revelation's readers: all the good things of Rev. 21:1-7 are intended for and belong to humanity as a whole, but this fact does not imply a promise of universal salvation. Those who demonstrate themselves unworthy of everlasting life will finally be removed from humanity and perish in the pool of fire, the second death (Rev. 20:7-10, 13-15).

Summary Remarks on Rev. 21:1-8

The glorious Parousia of God and Christ, popularly known as the Second Coming, signals the fulfillment of Christ's work of redeeming, maturing, and glorifying those who put faith in him. Those whom Jesus calls "children of the resurrection" (Lk. 20:36), whom John blesses as "those who have a part in the first resurrection" (Rev. 20:6; cf. Lk. 20:35), have grown up into

[114] NRSV has "the cross" in order to achieve gender inclusivity.

their inheritance as children of God, they have inherited the eternal life of God, they have inherited the restored and resurrected earth of God (Ps. 24:1; 1 Cor. 10:26), and they have taken up their part as co-regents of God on the earth (Rev. 5:10; 22:5; cf. Gen. 1:26-28). Their City, the New Jerusalem, belongs to the earth, and it belongs *on* the earth. When Jesus comes in glory to reign as Messiah, his faithful ones will be with him, they will conquer with him, and they will reign with him over the earth, the territory that he and they have conquered. They will join Jesus in his priestly role in relation to the living creation (Rev. 3:21; 5:10; 19:14; 20:4, 6; 22:5).

There is no good reason at all to split any of these promises from one another or from the Parousia as the occasion of their fulfillment. Rev. 21:1-8 belongs to the Parousia, pure and simple. The thousand-year imprisonment of the devil and the stubbornly unrepentant (Rev. 20:1-10; cf. Isa. 24:21–27:5; Mt. 25:41) has to do with the outworking of God's plan for dealing with *them*, and the period of their incarceration *does not logically require a delay in relation to any of the positive things that God has in store for the faithful.* The new creation naturally takes place at the Parousia, and the thousand-year reign of the faithful witnesses of God and Christ, no less than the rest of their unending reign that follows the thousand years (Rev. 20:4, 6; 22:5; cf. Dan. 7:18), naturally takes place in the new creation.

Chapter 2
Insurmountable Problems of Historic Premillennialism[1]

The exposition of Rev. 19:5–21:8 in Chapter 1 provides a demonstration of new creation millennialism's naturalness, its exegetical/explanatory power, its sensitivity to Revelation's richly allusive compositional style, and its handling of potential complications and difficulties. Presented positively and on its own, new creation millennialism *works* as an interpretive approach to Revelation 19–21. Chapters 2 and 3 will further demonstrate that this approach is "on track" by demonstrating that neither of the two most commonly employed interpretive solutions (premillennialism and amillennialism) stands up to examination as an alternative to new creation millennialism. I begin in this chapter by demonstrating the insurmountable problems of historic premillennialism. Historic premillennialism can be defined as having the following characteristics. Like new creation millennialism, (1) it reads Rev. 19:11-21 as a vision of the glorious Parousia of Christ, (2) it reads Rev. 20:1-3 and 20:4-6 as describing judgment events immediately connected with the Parousia, and (3) it reads Rev. 20:7-10 as describing events that happen after the end of the age that the Parousia inaugurates. Unlike new creation millennialism, (a) it reads Rev. 20:7-10 as picturing a rebellion of mortal people

[1] Dispensational or pretribulational interpretive schemes have their own independent difficulties, but they share all the fatal problems that I will be pointing out in relation to historic premillennialism. I will not be discussing dispensational premillennialism separately.

who have lived through the Parousia event, and/or their progeny born during the millennium, (b) it reads Rev. 20:11-15 as a single judgment scene that is distinct from and occurs after the rebellion of 20:7-10, and (c) it reads Rev. 21:1-4, the new creation and the coming-to-earth of the New Jerusalem, as occurring after the judgment of Rev. 20:11-15. It thus has the potential benefit of reading the text of Rev. 19:11–21:4 as a straightforward temporal sequence. But this is not an absolute benefit, because in Revelation, it cannot simply be assumed that what is narrated next comes next in the narrative world that lies behind the text. The reason for this is that in Revelation, John narrates a sequence of visions that he experienced, not a sequence of ordinary personal or historical events. What basis is there for assuming that if God or an angel brings a series of visions to a human being, the events symbolized or revealed in those visions must correspond, chronologically, with the order in which the visions are presented?

To take one obvious example, there is no way to dictate that John must only have one single vision of the Parousia of God and Christ. What if this world-upending event is full of more meaning than could ever be revealed in a single vision, or two visions, or even three visions? To open the door to the idea that the angel (Rev. 1:1) might show John more than one vision of the same event or reality is to dethrone the presupposition that a narrative text will always present scenes to us in simple chronological order. A proposed chronological reading must thus be able to answer, without special pleading, two key questions: (1) *Is it possible to read the text in simple chronological order without ignoring clear information in the text about what it means?* (2) *Is it possible to read the text in simple chronological order without running aground on major contradictions?* If the answer to either of these questions is negative, the simple chronological reading fails, and another reading strategy, based on other organizing principles in the text, must be sought. The following sections will demonstrate that historic premillennialism fails outright when confronted with each of these questions.

Who Survives the Transition to the Age to Come?

Historic premillennialism reads Rev. 20:7-10 and 20:11-15 as a simple chronological sequence. Therefore it does not, as new creation millennialism does, recognize 20:7-10 as narrating the resurrection of those refused resurrection in 20:4-5, and then recognize a second narration of, and a second viewpoint on, this resurrection and its results in 20:13-15. It thus identifies Gog and Magog (20:8) as nations made up of non-believers who have survived the Parousia (and their progeny born during the millennium). This identification becomes impossible when we realize that John repeatedly contradicts the assumption required here—that non-believers can in principle survive the Parousia.

For example, when John sees the Lamb open the sixth seal of the seven-sealed scroll in Rev. 6:12-17, he sees this scene:

> 12 I looked, and there came a great earthquake; the sun became black as sackcloth, the full moon became like blood, 13 and the stars of the sky fell to the earth as the fig tree drops its winter fruit when shaken by a gale. 14 The sky vanished like a scroll rolling itself up, and every mountain and island was removed from its place. 15 Then the kings of the earth and the magnates and the generals and the rich and the powerful, and **everyone, slave and free,** hid in the caves and among the rocks of the mountains, 16 calling to the mountains and rocks, "Fall on us and hide us from the face of the one seated on the throne and from the wrath of the Lamb; 17 for the great day of their wrath has come, and who is able to stand?"

The creation completely dissolves—stars fall down, the sky itself peels back like a reading scroll that splits in the middle, and all the features of the solid land move out of their places. "Everyone, slave and free," flees in terror (vv. 15-16), strongly evoking the scene of divine confrontation in Isaiah 2:10, 19, 21:

> 19 Enter the caves of the rocks
>   and the holes of the ground,
> from the terror of the LORD,
>   and from the glory of his majesty,
>   when he rises to terrify the earth.

Rev. 6:12-17 is the first of many scenes in Revelation depicting the coming in judgment of God and the Lamb. There is no need to describe this scene as "proleptic," as though it were somehow too early in the narrative to see a scene of the "End." On the contrary, the glorious Parousia of God and Christ stands as the central subject of Revelation. So much depth is packed into this subject that it cannot be revealed in a single vision-scene. John is going to see it and narrate it ten or more times, from many different angles.

The key point, in regard to Rev. 6:12-17, is that it depicts no room for earthly survivors in the great crisis of God's and Christ's intervention to judge humanity on the earth. *Everyone* on earth[2] is seen drawing back in fear and dread, even preferring for the mountains to fall on them and crush them rather than to face the arrival of the God who made them. This scene makes it very clear: if you're not with Jesus and God when they come, you're not going to survive meeting your Maker.

By contrast, the nearby scene in Rev. 7:9-17 shows what it looks like for people to *welcome* God and Jesus when they come in glory—but when an angel reveals the identity of the uncountable crowd of people waving palm branches and celebrating the arrival of God and his Christ, they turn out to be "they who have come out of the great ordeal [customarily "the great tribulation"]; they have washed their robes and made them white in the blood of the Lamb" (7:14). These are not non-Christians who have somehow managed to remain unrecruited by either Jesus or the Beast (whom readers will meet later) during the "the great ordeal," but rather those who have explicitly availed themselves of "the blood of the Lamb" to "wash their robes" and make them an acceptable welcoming party for God.

When readers do meet the Beast in Revelation 13, John makes it explicit that no one except "the saints," which is to say, the faithful and holy followers of Jesus, whom the Beast will attack

[2] We will find out in 19:14 (cf. 15:1-4) that those who belong to Christ will join him when he comes from heaven in glory to judge the world and to rule. They *do not* experience his Parousia standing on the earth (cf. similarly Mt. 24:29-31; Mk 13:24-27; 1 Thess. 4:13–5:3).

with deadly force, will avoid being drawn into the Beast's mandatory worship regime:

Rev. 13:7-8 (cf. vv. 15-17)

> 7 Also it was allowed to make war on the saints and to conquer them.[3] It was given authority over every tribe and people and language and nation, 8 and **all the inhabitants of the earth** will worship it, **everyone whose name has not been written from the foundation of the world in the book of life** of the Lamb that was slaughtered.[4]

John severely warns his readers that if you worship the Beast, you will suffer fiery torment when Jesus comes—and thus you will obviously not get to take part in the glorious age to come:

Rev. 14:9-10

> 9 Those who worship the beast and its image, and receive a mark on their foreheads or on their hands, 10 they will also drink the wine of God's wrath, poured unmixed into the cup of his anger, and they will be tormented with fire and sulfur in the presence of the holy angels and in the presence of the Lamb.

Finally, in the scene that serves as the gateway to Rev. 20:1-10, John again poses the total contrast between those who are with Jesus when he comes, on the one hand, and those who array themselves to oppose him:

Rev. 19:11-21

> 11 Then I saw heaven opened, and there was a white horse! Its rider is called Faithful and True, and in righteousness he judges and makes war. 12 His eyes are like a flame of fire, and on his head are many diadems; and he has a name inscribed that no one knows but himself. 13 He is clothed in a robe dipped in blood, and his name is called The Word of God. 14 And the armies of heaven, wearing fine linen, white and pure, were following him on white

[3] Some ancient manuscripts lack this sentence.

[4] Or, less likely, "written in the book of life of the Lamb that was slaughtered from the foundation of the world."

> horses. [15]From his mouth comes a sharp sword with which to strike down the nations, and he will rule them with a rod of iron; he will tread the wine press of the fury of the wrath of God the Almighty. [16]On his robe and on his thigh he has a name inscribed, "King of kings and Lord of lords."
>
> [17]Then I saw an angel standing in the sun, and with a loud voice he called to all the birds that fly in midheaven, "Come, gather for the great supper of God, [18]to eat the flesh of kings, the flesh of captains, the flesh of the mighty, the flesh of horses and their riders—flesh of **all, both free and slave, both small and great.**" [19]Then I saw the beast and the kings of the earth with their armies gathered to make war against the rider on the horse and against his army. [20]And the beast was captured, and with it the false prophet who had performed in its presence the signs by which he deceived those who had received the mark of the beast and those who worshiped its image. These two were thrown alive into the lake of fire that burns with sulfur. [21]And the rest were killed by the sword of the rider on the horse, the sword that came from his mouth; and all the birds were gorged with their flesh.

The beast and his armies fight to the death in order to keep Jesus from coming to reign as Lord and Christ, and they lose. John states in so many words that everyone on earth (at any rate, everyone who has survived the various crises of the great ordeal to take part in this final confrontation) joins the Beast in opposing Jesus and his army of the faithful (19:14), and that the former without exception perish in the battle for the earth (cf. "all," v. 17, and "the rest," v. 21).

Who, then, takes part in the age to come, when God, and Jesus, his Christ, come to reign in glory on the earth with their faithful ones (cf. Rev. 5:9-10; 11:18)? Only the faithful. No one else survives. Therefore, according to the narrative logic of Revelation itself, there is no room at all for the idea of an age that begins at Jesus Christ's coming in glory and has a population of ordinary mortals in addition to the resurrected faithful.

Some Revelation commentators attempt to solve this problem by proposing that Gog and Magog are to be understood as demonic, rather than human, forces. This approach, however, falls apart on the facts that (1) Gog and Magog are described as "the nations that are in the four corners of the earth" (Rev. 20:9), and (2) "the nations," whom the devil "comes out [of his underworld prison] to deceive" after the thousand years (20:7-8) must be the same nations he had previously been imprisoned in the underworld for a thousand years to keep him from deceiving (20:1-3). To say anything else is to throw textual coherence right out the window. The fact that scholars are willing swallow such a bitter pill of textual incoherence in order to avoid a "mixed" millennium reveals that to them the principle that only the faithful survive the Parousia in Revelation is absolutely unassailable.

Now that we've seen that the Book of Revelation is adamant that no one but the faithful survive Christ's coming in glory, let's see if there is any room in the thinking of Jesus and the New Testament writers for the idea of a mixed age following this one. First let's hear from Jesus:

Lk. 20:34-36

> 34 Jesus said to them, "Those who belong to this age marry and are given in marriage; 35 but those who are considered worthy of a place in that age and in the resurrection from the dead neither marry nor are given in marriage. 36 Indeed they cannot die anymore, because they are like angels and are children of God, being children of the resurrection.

According to Jesus, those considered worthy of taking part in the age to come are participants in "the resurrection from the dead," and they cannot die. This is an open-and-shut statement. Mortals will not have a part in the age to come; it is exclusively for "the children God," who are all "children of the resurrection." We'll have more to say about this passage later.

Now let's hear from Paul:

2 Thess. 1:7-10

> 6 For it is indeed just of God to repay with affliction those who afflict you, 7 and to give relief to the afflicted as well as to us, when the Lord Jesus is revealed from heaven with his mighty angels 8 in flaming fire, inflicting vengeance on those who do not know God and on those who do not obey the gospel of our Lord Jesus. 9 These will suffer the punishment of eternal destruction, separated from the presence of the Lord and from the glory of his might, 10 when he comes to be glorified by his saints and to be marveled at on that day among all who have believed, because our testimony to you was believed.

Paul here makes an absolute distinction between the fate of believers, on the one hand, and "those who don't know God" (v. 8), on the other. The believers will be glorified with Jesus, and will be amazed (with joy and admiration) to see him, whereas everyone else will experience "eternal destruction" (Gr. ὄλεθρος αἰώνιος). Paul here quotes from Isa. 2:10 (|| Isa. 2:19, 21) and Isa. 66:15-16 LXX:

> 10 Enter into the rock,
> and hide in the dust
> from the terror of the LORD,
> and from the glory of his majesty.

> 15 Look! The LORD is going to come like fire, and his chariots like a storm! He will deal out vengeance with wrath and a devastating rebuke in flaming fire. 16 For the whole earth is going to be judged by the fire of the LORD, and all flesh is going to be judged by his sword.

It is clear both from Paul's own language and from his use of Isaiah that he does not anticipate unbelievers surviving the Parousia.

Peter is, if anything, even more explicit and clear on this subject than Paul:

2 Pet. 3:5-13

> 5 ...by the word of God heavens existed long ago and an earth was formed out of water and by means of

> water, 6 through which the world of that time was deluged with water and perished. 7 But by the same word the present heavens and earth have been reserved for fire, being kept until the day of judgment and destruction of the godless.
>
> 8 But do not ignore this one fact, beloved, that with the Lord one day is like a thousand years, and a thousand years are like one day. 9 The Lord is not slow about his promise, as some think of slowness, but is patient with you,[5] not wanting any to perish, but all to come to repentance. 10 But the day of the Lord will come like a thief,[6] and then the heavens will pass away with a loud noise, and the elements will be dissolved with fire, and the earth and everything that is done on it will be disclosed.[7]
>
> 11 Since all these things are to be dissolved in this way, what sort of persons ought you to be in leading lives of holiness and godliness, 12 waiting for and hastening the coming of the day of God, because of which the heavens will be set ablaze and dissolved, and the elements will melt with fire?[8] 13 But, in accordance with his promise, we wait for new heavens and a new earth,[9] where righteousness is at home.

In this passage, as in 2 Thess. 1:7-10, the picture is of a radical judgment that comes on all of humanity, with the result that only two fates are possible: rescue and salvation for followers of Jesus on the one hand, or total, fiery destruction for the ungodly on the other hand. Peter goes so far as to make it

[5] This word is plural. Other ancient authorities read on your account.

[6] See Mt. 24:43-44; Lk. 12:39-40; see also 1 Thess. 5:2, 4; Rev. 3:3; 16:15.

[7] See Isa. 26:21. The mss are very divided about how this puzzling sentence should end: The oldest mss have "is going to be discovered"; other mss say "is going to be burned up completely"; some ancient translations have the word "not," producing "is *not* going to be discovered," i.e. "is not going to be found"; one has "is not going to appear"; one says "is going to be found disintegrated"; and a number of Greek mss and ancient translations simply leave all or part of the clause out altogether.

[8] Lit. "…God's day, because of which the heavens, burning, will disintegrate, and the elements, burning up, will melt."

[9] Isa. 65:17; 66:22.

explicit that the coming of "God's day" will see the radical destruction of the present created world and the establishment of a new heavens and a new earth (quoting Isa. 65:17; 66:22). There is no room, especially in this passage from 2 Peter, for the idea of ordinary flesh-and-blood people surviving to take part in the coming age of new creation.

Thus we find that Jesus, Paul, Peter, and the Book of Revelation all agree that no one will survive to take part in the age to come except the faithful. The mixed age pictured by historic pre-millennialism—in which ordinary mortals spared at Christ's coming share the earth with resurrected believers—is ruled out altogether.

One quibble that can be put to rest here is that Isaiah 65 mentions death in the age to come:

Isa. 65:17-20

> 17 For I am about to create new heavens
> and a new earth;
> the former things shall not be remembered
> or come to mind.
> 18 But be glad and rejoice forever
> in what I am creating;
> for I am about to create Jerusalem as a joy,
> and its people as a delight.
> 19 I will rejoice in Jerusalem,
> and delight in my people;
> no more shall the sound of weeping be heard in it,
> or the cry of distress.
> 20 No more shall there be in it
> an infant that lives but a few days,
> or an old person who does not live out a lifetime;
> for one who dies at a hundred years will be considered a youth,
> and one who falls short of a hundred will be considered accursed.

Whether one reads this passage from a point of view of trying to harmonize scripture with scripture, or whether one simply reads over John's shoulder to imagine how he might have read this passage harmonistically in relation to his own visions of the age to come, one thing remains impossible to overlook: The new creation and a divinely re-created Jerusalem (vv. 17, 18) establish the immediate context for the statement (v. 20) that appears to imply at least some degree of human mortality. If we do not wish to affirm on the basis of this prophecy that participants in the new creation and citizens of the New Jerusalem are subject to mortality (which would flatly contradict Rev. 21:4; cf. Lk. 20:36), then the obvious option for interpreting the passage is to say that it is hinting at something far greater—namely *resurrection and full immortality*—than the picture of a vastly extended human lifespan that it offers to the imagination of its readers (cf. Isa. 64:4; 1 Cor. 2:9; Col. 1:26-27). A reading of Isa. 65:20 must abandon the integrity of the text outright if it proposes either (1) to split Isaiah's description of greatly diminished mortality off from its context within the new creation or (2) to imagine that those subject to mortality might only be those who live *outside* the walls of the New Jerusalem. It is frankly a wrenching of Isaiah's words to pretend that he is saying either one of those things. If we are going to follow John in taking a harmonistic approach to the prophetic scriptures at all, then we are going to have to say that Isaiah 65 hints at, but understates, the blessing of full immortality that will be the experience of all who are invited to take part in the New Jerusalem of God and the New Creation of God.[10]

[10] It seems reasonable to conjecture that John would have taken a similar progressive revelation approach to the prophecy of Zech. 14:12-19—which, unlike Isaiah 65–66, he does not allude to anywhere in Revelation. A possible elaboration of this conjecture (from an OT–NT harmonistic perspective) is to propose that the LXX of Zech. 14:17 may correctly reflect the Hebrew original, which would thus have read, "If any of the tribes of the earth do not go up to Jerusalem to worship the King, the Lord almighty, these will be added to those." That is, Zechariah seems originally to have prophesied that all those who do not go up to fight against Jerusalem but who nonetheless refuse to worship the Lord almighty, will experience the same instant destruction as those who actively attacked Jerusalem (see 14:12). Thus, in the LXX version of conditions in the age of the Lord's kingship over all the earth (14:9), it is not only true to say that some from the Gentiles will be accepted by God when God comes in glory to reign on earth, but also that there will be no one anywhere on earth who does not go up to worship God. It will be an age which only willing worshipers from all nations will survive to enjoy. If the LXX of Zech. 14:7 does reflect the original Hebrew, the Hebrew

When Does the New Creation Take Place?

When does the new creation take place according to the Book of Revelation? We don't have explicit chronological statements to answer this question for us, but we do have a number of kinds of information from which the answer can consistently be inferred. The first point to make is that, without specific and compelling indications in the text that we should split them apart, the coming of the new creation must be presumed to be associated with the dissolution of the present creation. Dissolution and re-creation, in other words, are naturally assumed to form a complex. The creation requires *re-creation* because it perishes; conversely, the creation is disintegrated in order to pave the way for its reconstruction. Secondly, the coming of the New Jerusalem is intimately associated with the renewal of the creation (Rev. 21:1-2), therefore indicators as to the timing of the coming of the New Jerusalem will also serve equally as indicators of the timing of the new creation.

When, then, does the *dissolution* of the present creation occur according to the Book of Revelation? We've seen above that it is associated with the Parousia of God and Jesus Christ (Rev. 6:12-17). Other passages in Revelation underline this. For example, after the seventh trumpet the elders prophesy,

Rev. 11:17-18

> 17 We give you thanks, Lord God Almighty,
> who are and who were,[11]
> for you have taken your great power
> and begun to reign.
> 18 The nations raged,
> but your wrath has come,
> and the time for judging the dead,
> for rewarding your servants, the prophets
> and saints and all who fear your name,

Masoretic Text can be seen to agree with Targum Pseudo-Jonathan in trying to make a meaningful story out of the puzzlingly terse original, "these will be added to those" (v. 17), by imagining that God will *force* recalcitrant nations to go up to Jerusalem to worship in the age of his kingdom, by withholding rain from them until they do.

[11] Lit. "the Is and the Was." See Rev. 1:8; 4:8.

> both small and great,
> and for destroying those who destroy the earth.

This announcement comes as part of the seventh trumpet—which, as the seventh and final element in its series, naturally asks to be interpreted as the great judgment of the living and the dead that accompanies Christ's coming in glory. John's readers have seen a third of humanity and a third of the living creation (including a third of marine life) destroyed after the sounding of the previous trumpets (8:6–9:19); eventually they will see all marine life (16:3) and all humanity (19:21) perish as well. Rev. 11:18 indicates that the reason for God and Christ's intervention is that godless humanity is in the process of destroying all life on earth. This moment of intervention, to rescue the earth from its destruction by humanity (cf. Mt. 24:22: Mk 13:20), becomes a natural moment for God to heal, restore, and re-create the earth.

Later on, the seventh (and final) bowl scene, with its unparalleled and civilization-destroying earthquake and its narration of the fleeing of all mountains and islands, certainly underlines the idea that God's coming will see the dissolution of the present, damaged creation:

Rev. 16:17-20

> 17 The seventh angel poured his bowl into the air, and a loud voice came out of the temple, from the throne, saying, "It is done!" 18 And there came flashes of lightning, rumblings, peals of thunder, and a violent earthquake, such as had not occurred since people were upon the earth, so violent was that earthquake. 19 The great city was split into three parts, and the cities of the nations fell. God remembered great Babylon and gave her the wine-cup of the fury of his wrath. 20 And every island fled away, and no mountains were to be found.

Finally, as John begins to narrate his "Great White Throne Judgment" vision, John refers back to these sweeping scenes of transition and dissolution in the following words:

Rev. 20:11 (my translation)

> [11] And I saw a great white throne, and the One who sat on it—he from whose presence earth and heaven fled away, and no room was found for them.

As we saw in Chapter 1, the description of the Enthroned One points us back both to Rev. 6:14—in which we saw the sky snapping apart like a worn-out papyrus scroll that splits in the middle, and the largest-scale geological features of the earth slipping around—and to the equally radical Rev. 16:17-20, which we just read above. Both of these scenes of cosmic disruption are to be understood as pictures of the Parousia of God and the Lamb. In Rev. 20:11 John is referring back to the previous scenes in which he saw God appear as Judge, and he is characterizing what he has seen in his visions as a fleeing away and disappearance of earth and heaven, or, in other words, as a complete disintegration of the present creation. In the absence of clear textual indications to the contrary, the assumption must be that the creation *dissolved* at the coming of God and Christ now needs to be *re-created*, and that it will indeed be re-created. Why? Because the Creator, who is also the God of the Renewal of All Things (Rev. 21:5), has come to reign on the earth.

Moreover, as I argued in the exposition, *John does not narrate* in Rev. 20:11 that earth and heaven fled—as though the scene of Rev. 20:11-15 were straightforwardly to be understood as taking place after the events of 20:7-10. English translations almost always understand the Greek relative clause in v. 11 (οὗ ἀπὸ προσώπου ἔφυγεν ἡ γῆ καὶ ὁ οὐρανός) as narrating the fleeing of earth and heaven. Two facts combine to rule out this interpretation, however. First, the Greek relative pronoun οὗ, translated as "whose," lies *outside* the prepositional phrase. This results in the sense, "…and sitting upon it was he from whose presence earth and heaven fled," rather than, as it is typically rendered, "…and him who sat upon it. From his presence earth and heaven fled." Secondly, the grammatical dynamics of the relative clause in 20:11 are those of a resumptive description rather than of a narration of unfolding events. As noted above in the exposition of Rev. 20:11, examination of the 66 other relative clauses in the visionary portion of Revelation (Rev. 1:9–22:17) reveals that *not one of them* carries narrative action in the way that would be demanded by the familiar translation of 20:11. John's relative clauses in his vision narrative *always* fill a descriptive or identifying role, and *never* carry the weight of the vision narrative.[12]

In summary, John's visions picture the dissolution of the present creation as an aspect of the Parousia of God and Christ, the crisis point that ends the present age and inaugurates the age to come. Two implications arise from this. First, the dissolution of the earth at the Parousia double-underlines the principle that no mortal person survives the Parousia. No ordinary human being can survive heaven and earth fleeing away. Secondly, the expectation will be that the re-creation, the renewal, the resurrection, of the cosmos also belongs at the same moment.[13] However, this cannot simply be assumed without further demonstration. Ideally, it would be good to be able to lay our hands on clear positive evidence in Revelation that the re-creation itself is to be understood as occurring at the Parousia. This we will discover by looking at the timing of the coming to earth of the New Jerusalem, since Rev. 21:1-2 indicates that this happens in the context of the renewed, re-created cosmos.

When Does the New Jerusalem Come to Earth?

A first line of evidence as to the timing of the coming-to-earth of the New Jerusalem grows out of the consistency of the pattern that joins the promises to "those who conquer" in the letters to the angels of the seven churches (Rev. 2–3). Each letter holds out hopes of things to be received or fully experienced when Jesus comes again in glory. For example,

Rev. 2:7

> [7] To everyone who conquers, I will give permission to eat from the tree of life that is in the paradise of God.

[12] For a fuller discussion of this technical translation issue, see Mealy, *After the Thousand Years* (see p. 10 nt. 1 above), 162-67.
[13] Jesus (Mt. 19:28) and Paul (Rom. 8:18-23) both say things indicating that the renewal of the creation takes place when Jesus comes in glory. More will be said about this below.

Access to the tree of life represents the gift of resurrection and immortality, which the overcomers will receive when Jesus comes again (see also Rev. 22:1-5).

Rev. 2:10

> 10 Be faithful until death, and I will give you the crown of life.

The "crown of life" represents resurrection, which Jesus will give to the faithful as a reward at his coming.

Rev. 2:17

> 17 To everyone who conquers I will give some of the hidden manna,[14] and I will give a white stone, and on the white stone is written a new name that no one knows except the one who receives it.[15]

The "hidden manna" is Jesus himself, who is himself the source and sustenance of eternal life. Although he is now hidden in heaven, the true ark of the covenant, he will no longer be hidden when he comes again to reign (cf. Jn 6:32-58; Rev. 11:19; Exod. 16:33; Heb. 9:4).

Rev. 2:26-28

> 26 To everyone who conquers and continues to do my works to the end, I will give authority over the nations;
> 27 To rule [lit. *shepherd*] them with an iron rod—
> as when clay pots are shattered—[16]
>
> 28 even as I also received authority from my Father. To the one who conquers I will also give the morning star.[17]

Verses 26 and 27 here promise the overcomers that they will be victorious with Jesus when he wins possession of the earth from the hostile and godless. We see this participation of the faithful with Jesus at his Parousia in Rev. 19:14-15. The gift of the

[14] See Exod. 16, esp. v. 33.
[15] See e.g. Zech. 3:8-9.
[16] Ps. 2:8-9. This militaristic language is going to be interpreted later as the conquering power of testifying to the truth (e.g. Rev. 19:11-15).
[17] That is, the gift of himself: Rev. 22:16.

"morning star" (v. 28) is also, of course, a promise of receiving Jesus himself at his coming (cf. Rev. 22:16).

Rev. 3:5

> 5 If you conquer, you will be clothed like them in white robes, and I will not blot your name out of the book of life; I will confess your name before my Father and before his angels.[18]

Jesus here refers to the judgment of all humanity that will take place at his Parousia with God, and in which those who have conducted themselves honorably in his name in their mortal lives will be vindicated and invited to take part in the age to come (cf. Rev. 3:4, 18; 7:9, 13-15; 19:7-8, 14; 20:4-6).

Rev. 3:21

> 21 To the one who conquers I will give a place with me on my throne, just as I myself conquered and sat down with my Father on his throne.

When will the "conquerors" (which is to say, those who remain faithful to death, Rev. 12:11) reign with Jesus? The simple and expected answer is, "at his Parousia, when he comes with his Father to reign on the earth." The vision-scene that follows the sounding of the seventh trumpet underlines the idea that the Parousia of God and Jesus Christ is *the unique occasion* for rewards to be given to the faithful:

Rev. 11:15-18; cf. Rev. 5:10;[19] 20:4-6

> 15 Then the seventh angel blew his trumpet, and there were loud voices in heaven, saying,

[18] See Exod. 32:32-33; Ps. 69:28; Dan. 12:1.

[19] The textual variant "they reign on the earth" in 5:10 presents a thorny problem. Bruce Metzger comments on this verse, "It is … difficult to choose between βασιλεύσουσιν ["they will reign"], supported by ℵP 1 94 1854 2053 2344 it^{gig} vg syr^{ph} cop$^{sa, bo}$ arm *al*, and βασιλεύουσιν ["they reign"], supported by A 046 1006 1611 it^{61} syr^{h} *al*. A majority of the Committee, noting that in 20:6 codex Alexandrinus mistakenly reads βασιλεύουσιν for the future tense, preferred βασιλεύσουσιν here, as more suited to the meaning of the context" (*A Textual Commentary on the Greek New Testament: A Companion Volume to the United Bible Societies' Greek New Testament* (3rd edn; New York and

> "The kingdom of the world has become the kingdom of
> our Lord
> and of his Messiah,
> and he will reign forever and ever."

> 16 Then the twenty-four elders who sit on their thrones before God fell on their faces and worshiped God, 17 singing,

> "We give you thanks, Lord God Almighty,
> who are and who were,[20]
> for you have taken your great power
> and begun to reign.
> 18 The nations raged,
> but your wrath has come,
> and the time for judging the dead,
> for rewarding your servants, the prophets
> and saints and all who fear your name,
> both small and great,
> and for destroying those who destroy the earth."

Just as Jesus took up his reign at his resurrection, so the natural expectation is that the faithful will be rewarded with the honor of reigning alongside him at their resurrection, which accompanies his coming.

Rev. 3:12

> 12 If you conquer, I will make you a pillar in the temple of my God; you will never go out of it. I will write on you the name of my God, and the name of the city of my God, the new Jerusalem that comes down from my God out of heaven, and my own new name.[21]

In Revelation, the true Temple of God is now in heaven (4:5-8 [cf. Isa. 6:1-3]; 11:19; 12:12; 13:6; 15:5-8; 16:17). The True/New Jerusalem is also now in heaven—in fact, it is fair to

Stuttgart: United Bible Societies, 1975). I agree with Metzger and the Committee.

[20] Lit. "the Is and the Was." See Rev. 1:8; 4:8.

[21] This alludes to Jer. 23:6; 33:15-16. All three names are one name: YHWH (is) Our Vindication.

say that the two (City and Temple) ultimately represent one reality: the community of the faithful, who worship and serve God in his intimate presence. This identity between the true Temple and the New Jerusalem is brought into sharper focus by the fact that, when the New Jerusalem comes down from heaven in Rev. 21:2, 10-11, John says, "I saw no temple in the city, for its temple is the Lord God the Almighty and the Lamb" (21:22). No temple building can be seen in "the Holy City" (21:9), whose very dimensions and materials tell us that it, as a whole, constitutes the ultimate "Holy of Holies"—just like the Holy of Holies in Solomon's Temple, the entire New Jerusalem is a cube of pure gold (cf. Rev. 21:18; 1 Kgs 6:20; 2 Chron. 3:8). Just as God's tent/temple in heaven symbolizes "those who dwell in heaven" (Rev. 13:6; cf. 11:19; 14:15, 17; 15:5; 21:3, 22), so the New Jerusalem that John describes in Rev. 21:2; 21:9–22:5 symbolizes the people of God on earth in the age to come,[22] over whom God will pitch his tent of total, intimate presence forever (Rev. 21:3; cf. Rev. 7:15; Isa. 4:5-6; 25:4).

When will this final dwelling of God with and in his people on earth be fulfilled? When will the hidden, heavenly Jerusalem (Gal. 4:26; Phil. 3:20; Heb. 12:22), the community of the faithful, become manifest, and take up its place on the earth? Absent strong and clear textual indications to the contrary, the answer to this question should be assumed to be consistent with the pattern I have just demonstrated among all the other promises to the overcomers in the seven letters: at the glorious Parousia of God and Jesus. This consistent pattern among the letters does not constitute ironclad proof in and of itself, but it does carry real and substantial weight. This weight would have to be counterbalanced by other, equally forceful, considerations *militating against* the coming to earth of the New Jerusalem at the Parousia, in order for us to consider the possibility that John wishes us to imagine an age-long delay intervening between the Parousia and the coming of the New Jerusalem. Moreover, when we frame the question a slightly different way, evidence comes to hand that essentially *proves* that the coming of the New Jerusalem and the Parousia belong together.

[22] See, correctly, R. H. Gundry, "The New Jerusalem: People as Place, not Place for People." *Novum Testamentum* 29 (1987) 254-64.

When Does the Wedding between Jesus and the New Jerusalem, His Bride, Take Place?

In order to answer this question, we need to look a little more deeply into how narrative progress is accomplished in Revelation 19–21. In doing this we are going to be able to show that the pattern of textual progress in these three chapters fits into the consistent way in which the text progresses from 4:1 (John's invitation to heaven) onwards.

The Wedding of Jesus Christ, the Warrior King

In Revelation 19:6-9, a great crowd in heaven loudly celebrates two things that go together: the coming of the Reign of God, and the Wedding of the Lamb and his Bride:

Rev. 19:6-9

> 6 Then I heard what seemed to be the voice of a great multitude, like the sound of many waters and like the sound of mighty thunderpeals, crying out,
>
> "Hallelujah!
> For the Lord our God
> the Almighty reigns.
> 7 Let us rejoice and exult
> and give him the glory,
> for the marriage of the Lamb has come,
> and his bride has made herself ready;
> 8 to her it has been granted to be clothed
> with fine linen, bright and pure"—
>
> for the fine linen is the righteous deeds of the saints.
>
> 9 And the angel said to me, "Write this: Blessed are those who are invited to the marriage supper of the Lamb." And he said to me, "These are true words of God."

In the following section, Rev. 19:11-21, we will see Jesus coming as the Messianic Warrior King. Using the sole weapon of his testimony to the truth, symbolized by the sword that John sees coming out of his mouth, Jesus will conquer and cast out the violent would-be possessors of the earth. The two sections—the announcement of the wedding and the scene of

Christ's victorious conquest of the earth—are tied together by their common scriptural background in Psalm 45, which blesses the conquering warrior king and praises the beauty of his bride-to-be on their wedding day. In Revelation 19, the wedding day of Christ and the faithful is at the same time the day of their joint victory (v. 14) over the forces of violence and destruction.

Revelation 20: Two Interlocking Pairs of Visions

Revelation 20 carries the visionary narrative forward by means of two interlocked pairs of visions (see Figure 1 below). One pair of visions reveals the age-long imprisonment, the release and resurgence, and the final destruction of the devil and the unrepentant (20:1-3, 7-10). The other pair of visions unpacks the intertwined themes of resurrection and judgment. The first vision of the latter pair (20:4-6) reveals the world judgment (cf. Dan. 7:10-14, 18, 26-27), which results in the choosing of the faithful witnesses of God and Jesus for resurrection and reign, at the same time decreeing refusal of resurrection for the "rest of the dead" (20:5; cf. Isa. 26:14-19). The second vision of that pair (20:11-15) reveals not only the negative side of the world judgment (v. 12; cf. v. 4 as the positive side), but also the ultimate resurrection, judgment, and destruction of those found unworthy of resurrection at "the first resurrection" (vv. 13-15).

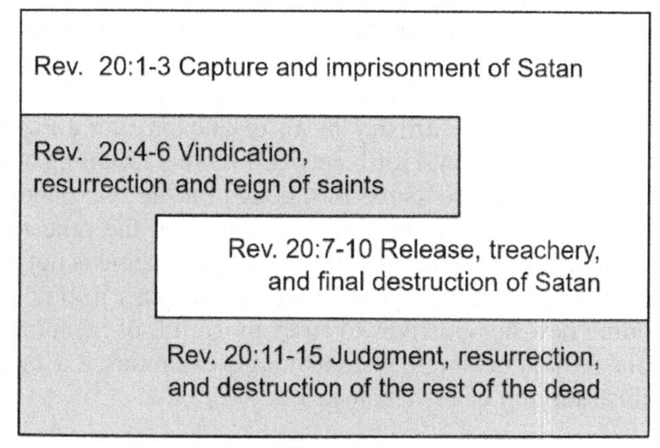

Figure 1

The foregoing synopsis of Revelation 20 shows that it wraps up the particular themes of (1) the judgment and final disposition of Satan (20:1-3, 7-10), (2) the judgment of the faithful, resulting in vindication and resurrection (20:4-6), and (3) the judgment of the unrepentant, resulting in conviction and punishment (20:11-15). In terms of narrative progress, Revelation 20 carries forward these three themes to their final conclusion. It does not, however, advance the previously announced theme of the marriage of Christ and his Bride (19:6-9). The explication, elaboration, and conclusion of this theme awaits its resumption in Rev. 21:1-2.

Revelation 21:1-8: Its Function Within the Vision Narrative

The assumption that we must evaluate at this point—rather than take for granted—is whether Revelation is composed in such a way as to lead us to the presumption that anything narrated in Rev. 21:1 will belong to the time period *after* the final resurrection and judgment of the unrepentant narrated in 20:13-15. *If* Revelation were composed according to the most-often-used habits of ancient storytelling, the answer to this would clearly be affirmative. In the ancient and classical worlds, stories are usually told sequentially: they begin at a starting point (even if that point is in the middle of the overall story, *in medias res*), they advance through time with occasional flashbacks, digressions, and foreshadowings, and they finish at some kind of temporal end point. Revelation, however, does not follow this pattern at all. Revelation, the single most sophisticated example of narrative artistry in all of ancient literature, constantly shuttles back and forth between visions revealing human sinfulness and unrepentance in this age on the one hand, and visions of the Parousia of God and Christ on the other hand. Narrative progress in relation to the Parousia theme is not made by moving along to "the next thing that happens in time," but by adding new perspectives to an event so full of meaning and complexity that no single vision could ever capture it. Consider the illustration in Chart 1 below.

Chart 1[23]

[23] This basic chart plots the flow of the Revelation main vision narrative text in chapters 4–22 (see the word count at the bottom, running from left to right) against the temporal aspect of the subject matter at each point. Higher on the page indicates further along in time. See Appendix 1 for the narrative analysis that lies behind the chart.

Chart 1 illustrates the fact that the Revelation vision narrative keeps cycling between descriptions of the distresses and judgments that lead to the end of the current age, and descriptions of the Parousia of God and Christ. I think it is reasonable to assume that there is some temporal progress through the narrative towards the final end of this age, in that the sequences of the seals, trumpets, and bowls are evidently intended to be understood as focusing on events progressively closer to the Parousia in time. Nonetheless, the overall temporal progress is not in any way linear, because new Parousia visions repeatedly intervene between judgment episodes. This consistent pattern suggests that there are *two* initially feasible ways of taking the new creation and New Jerusalem scene in Rev. 21:1-8. On the one hand, we can read it in standard narrative processing mode, as depicting the situation that comes into being after the final, post-millennial judgment of the unrepentant depicted in Rev. 20:13-15. On the other hand, we can equally well read it as cycling back again from a judgment scene to the presentation of yet another viewpoint on the Parousia of God and Christ. The two dashed lines showing for Rev. 21:1–22:5 in the chart above illustrate that, in view of the consistent chronological pattern that precedes it, the new creation scene is just as capable of being understood as belonging chronologically to the Parousia as to the period after the final judgment of the unrepentant. *Considerations other than its sequential position in the text must dictate its temporal plotting.*

Let us, then, consider the positive evidence that the coming of the new creation and the New Jerusalem in Rev. 21:1-8 reveals yet another aspect of the Parousia of God and the Lamb.

First, as noted above, the appearance of the New Jerusalem as the bride resumes the theme of the wedding and the wedding banquet announced in Rev. 19:6-9. To the extent that we understand the thousand years of Rev. 20:1-10 as inaugurated by the Parousia, we have to ask what point there would be in announcing the messianic wedding in connection with the Parousia in 19:6-9, if the wedding were not intended to be understood as revealing an aspect of the Parousia itself. In the rest of the NT as well as Revelation, Christ's coming in glory is represented as the consummation of the spiritual union between Christ and his faithful. Symbolically speaking, the community of the faithful is already in this age in the betrothal period with Christ (cf. Rev. 22:17; 2 Cor. 11:2; Eph. 5:23-32), so there seems to be no conceivable rationale for an age-long wait *after* the Parousia for the marriage itself. On this logic, the coming of the New Jerusalem adorned as the Bride of Christ on her wedding day (21:2) practically demands to be understood as a vision of the Parousia.

Secondly, although John does not make a lot of it, he has already reported seeing the "the Beloved City" on the earth at the end of the thousand years in Rev. 20:9. This—at least on a premillennial interpretation—should lead us to the straightforward conclusion that the New Jerusalem, Christ's beloved bride, has already been established on the earth at the Parousia.

Thirdly, as outlined above, the idea that the coming down to earth of the New Jerusalem happens at the Parousia brings the promise to the faithful at Philadelphia in Rev. 3:11-12 completely into line with the promises that conclude the letters to all the other churches. All seven promises point to good gifts that the faithful will receive from their Savior when he comes again.

Fourthly, the whole idea of the Parousia of God and the Lamb is that a moment will arrive when they will no longer reign from heaven, but will from then on reign on the earth—along with their faithful ones (cf. 5:10; 11:15-19; 14:1-5).[24] The *coming down from heaven* of the New Jerusalem thus paints a perfectly congruent picture of this coming as regards the role of the faithful, and the words that follow the announcement of the coming of the New Jerusalem in Rev. 21:2 confirm that *God himself comes with her* to make his permanent abode on earth with her. The words of Rev. 21:3-6 not only make this explicit, but also strikingly recall the words that the angel uses in Rev. 7:15-17 when he explains the Parousia scene that John has just witnessed in Rev. 7:9-12:

[24] This coming of God's reign from heaven to earth is, of course, exactly what Jesus himself instructs his followers to pray for: "Your kingdom come—your will be done on earth as it is in heaven!"

[3] *...See, the home [lit. tent] of God is among mortals.*
He will dwell [lit. live in a tent] with them;
they will be his people[s],
and God himself will be with them;
[4] **he will wipe every tear from their eyes.**
Death will be no more;
mourning and crying and pain will be no more,
for the first things have passed away."

[5] And the one who was seated on the throne said, "See, I am making all things new." Also he said, "Write this, for these words are trustworthy and true." [6] Then he said to me, "It is done! I am the Alpha and the Omega, the beginning and the end. To the thirsty I will give water as a gift from the spring of the water of life.

[15] **For this reason they are before the throne of God,**

and worship him day and night within his temple,

and the one who is seated on the throne will shelter [lit. put up his tent over] them.

[16] They will hunger no more, and thirst no more;

the sun will not strike them,

nor any scorching heat;

[17] for the Lamb at the center of the throne will be their shepherd,

and he will guide them to springs of the water of life,

and **God will wipe away every tear from their eyes.**

It now remains to summarize the cumulative force of all the foregoing evidence, as regards the temporal plotting of the new creation in Revelation. (1) The visions of the sixth seal (Rev. 6:12-17), the seventh trumpet (Rev. 11:15-19), the seventh bowl (Rev. 16:17-21), and Rev. 20:11 make it clear that the dissolution, the disintegration, of the present creation attends the Parousia of God and Christ. (2) In the absence of clear and explicit textual evidences to the contrary, the presumption must be that the healing, the renewal, the resurrection of the creation as a whole (like that of the faithful) also attends the Parousia of God and Christ. (3) The coming down to earth of the Bride, the New Jerusalem, clearly attends the Parousia of God and Christ, and is inseparably linked to the coming of the new creation (Rev. 21:1-2). Therefore (4) the new creation in the Book of Revelation is undoubtedly to be understood as attending the Parousia of God and Christ.

Jesus, Paul, and Peter on the Renewal of the Creation

Let us now turn to the teachings of Jesus, Paul, and Peter to see whether they too look forward to the radical renewal of the creation at the Parousia.

Mt. 19:28

> 28 Jesus said to them, "Truly I tell you, at the renewal of all things, when the Son of Man is seated on the throne of his glory, you who have followed me will also sit on twelve thrones, judging the twelve tribes of Israel."[25]

It is not absolutely certain that Jesus ever directly addresses the idea of a "new creation," but *if he does*, this statement is his clearest reference to it. He appears to be indicating here that he expects his glorious coming as the Son of Man (which is to say, "The Human One," Gr. ὁ υἱὸς τοῦ ἀνθρώπου, cf. Dan. 7:13-14, 18, 26-27) to be associated with the regeneration, the rebirth, of the creation. Admittedly, the word παλιγγενεσία has a range of possible applications, including the rebirth of the world after the flood[26] and the rebirth of Israel after the exile,[27] as well as the rebirth of the person who has become renewed by the Holy Spirit as a Christian (Tit. 3:5). A majority of interpreters do, however, understand Mt. 19:28 as referring to the regeneration of the cosmos at the transition between this age and the age of resurrection that follows this age.[28]

[25] Closely parallel to this passage is Mt. 25:31: "When the Son of Man comes in his glory, and all the angels with him, then he will sit on the throne of his glory."

[26] See Philo, *Vit. Mos.* 2.65.

[27] E.g. Josephus, *Ant.* 11.66.

[28] For a judicious discussion, see R.T. France, *The Gospel of Matthew* (NICCNT; Grand Rapids: Eerdmans, 2007), p. 742-43.

Let's now hear from Paul:

Rom. 8:18-23

> 18 I consider that the sufferings of this present time are not worth comparing with the glory about to be revealed to us. 19 For the creation waits with eager longing for the revealing of the children of God; 20 for the creation was subjected to futility,[29] not of its own will but by the will of the one who subjected it, in hope 21 that the creation itself will be set free from its bondage to decay and will obtain the freedom of the glory of the children of God. 22 We know that the whole creation has been groaning in labor pains until now; 23 and not only the creation, but we ourselves, who have the first fruits of the Spirit, groan inwardly while we wait for adoption, the redemption of our bodies.

This passage is the closest that Paul comes to speaking explicitly about a cosmic new creation. Given the analogy that he is assuming between human mortality and the "bondage to decay" to which the whole creation has been subjected because of us (vv. 20-21), it seems clear that Paul believes the whole living creation will experience something analogous to our resurrection at the same time that we experience resurrection—which he here calls "the redemption of our bodies" (v. 23). Our mortality is linked to the mortality (described as "decay," or "corruption"[30]) of the living creation; our yearning is linked to the yearning of all creation; our setting free from mortality is linked to the setting free of the whole creation from corruption. Paul clearly expects our resurrection to attend the coming of Jesus, ergo Paul expects the renewal, the resurrection, of the whole creation to attend the coming of Jesus.

Here is what Peter has to say:

2 Pet. 3:11-13

> 11 Since all these things are to be dissolved in this way, what sort of persons ought you to be in leading lives of

[29] Or "vanity," or "human foolishness."

[30] Gr. φθορά.

> holiness and godliness, 12 waiting for and hastening[31] the coming of the day of God, because of which the heavens will be set ablaze and dissolved, and the elements will melt with fire? 13 But, in accordance with his promise, we wait for new heavens and a new earth, where righteousness is at home.[32]

Peter simply and directly associates the fiery disintegration of the present cosmos *and* the coming of "a new heavens and a new earth" with the "arrival of God's day," which, in the context, is clearly identical with "the day of the Lord," and with "his [i.e. the Lord Jesus'] coming," which Peter sees as the end-point of this current age (2 Pet. 3:3-9).

Concluding Remarks: Implications—and Non-Implications—of These Findings

I suspect that a significant number of my readers are now saying to themselves, "Doesn't Mealy realize that he's just presented an ironclad case in favor of amillennialism?" I fully admit to have presented an ironclad case *against* historic premillennialism, with its unsupportable concept of an age-long delay between the Parousia of God and Christ on the one hand, and the coming to earth of the New Jerusalem, the wedding of the Lamb and the Bride, and the new creation, on the other hand. But the evidence I have presented in no way amounts to a proof of amillennialism. The decisive question in relation to amillennialism—the question of whether the thousand years of Rev. 20:1-10 *begins* or *ends* at the Parousia of God and Christ—remains entirely separate. And that question has a very clear answer. In the following chapter I will demonstrate that attempts to read Rev. 20:1-10 so as to interpret the thousand years as the period before the Parousia inevitably result in fatal narrative incoherence.

[31] Or *earnestly desiring*

[32] Isa. 65:17; 66:22.

Chapter 3
Insurmountable Problems with Amillennialism

Candid amillennialist exegetes will sometimes concede that an amillennialist reading of Rev. 20:1-10 arises not from a reading of the passage itself but from a pair of firm preconceptions drawn from outside of the passage, and indeed, from outside the Book of Revelation altogether.[1] The first preconception is that there is no New Testament evidence (outside the contested Rev. 20:4-6) for the belief that the coming of Christ will be accompanied not by a general resurrection to judgment, but rather by a selective resurrection that benefits the faithful alone. I will demonstrate in Chapter 4 that this first preconception is flatly mistaken. The second preconception—with which I have no quarrel—is that Scripture always agrees with itself. My observation, based on reading something on the order of three hundred books and articles touching the subject of the millennium, is that only those who bring *both* of these a priori commitments to the passage find themselves tempted to cast about for a reading in which the end—and not the beginning—of the thousand years is made to correspond temporally with the Parousia of God and Christ.[2] An amillennial interpretation, in

[1] See, e.g., R. Reymond, *A New Systematic Theology of the Christian Faith* (2nd edn; New York: Thos. Nelson, 1997), mcccxl-mcccxli.
[2] Revelation scholars with no overriding commitment to the infallibility of Scripture find little difficulty in allowing for the possibility that John's chronological scheme of resurrection and judgment will differ significantly from that found elsewhere in the New Testament. Such scholars typically take

other words, only arises when interpreters bring an *external agenda* to their reading of the passage. This ought to send up a cautionary flag right from the start. Be that as it may, I would like to call attention to three separate and independently significant problems with an amillennial reading of Revelation 20.[3] In my judgment the first problem makes an amillennial reading distinctly improbable, and each of the last two independently makes an amillennial reading outright impossible.

First Problem: When Resurrection Does Not Equal Resurrection

This problem is quite serious, but it is not necessarily fatal to amillennialism all by itself. I mention it first because it is the least of the three problems that I will discuss. I begin with a point that may seem almost too obvious to mention here: John belongs to and writes for a Christian community whose members hold, as their central hope for the future, the hope of bodily resurrection to everlasting life. From the first generation of believers onward, the achievement of this hope has always been connected to the Parousia of Jesus. Thus in Rev. 20:4, 6 John is not only using the familiar Christian language of resurrection, but he is using it *in a context in which a reference to the literal, physical resurrection of believers would naturally be expected.* After all, we have just seen Revelation's most dramatic vision

a premillennial interpretation, which is to say, they read the scenes of Rev. 20:1-10 as following on from the scene of Rev. 19:11-21.

[3] There are several more problems, such as the fact that the slain martyrs who cry out in heaven for vindication in Rev. 6:9-11 are *told to rest quietly and to wait for their vindication* until the full number of their fellow martyrs has been reached, whereas Rev. 20:4 pictures the vindication of *all* the martyrs by the heavenly court, with the result that they are pictured as coming to life and actively reigning with Christ. An amillennial reading usually forces the interpreter to treat what looks like a dramatic story sequence (passive rest and waiting in heaven during this age of continued martyrdom, then finally resurrection and active reign on earth of all the martyrs at the Parousia) as a paradoxical double view on the same (intermediate, unresurrected) state. Problems of this order, however, will appear relatively minor in comparison to the ones I will be discussing.

of the Parousia in 19:11-21.[4] Accordingly, anyone who wishes to assert that John is referring in Rev. 20:4, 6 to something besides bodily resurrection[5] assumes a heavy burden of proof. But beyond that, here is the *real* problem.

In Rev. 20:4 John writes that he watched as the souls of those beheaded by the beast "came to life" (ἔζησαν)[6] and reigned with Christ for **the** thousand years (καὶ ἐβασίλευσαν μετὰ Χριστοῦ **τὰ** χίλια ἔτη), namely the thousand years just mentioned both in 20:2 and 20:3. In 20:5 he says, in reference to this coming to life and reigning, "this is the first resurrection" (αὕτη ἡ ἀνάστασις ἡ πρώτη). The rest of the dead, he says, "did not come to life again" (οὐκ ἀνέζησαν) until the thousand years were completed.

Any coherent reading of Rev. 20:4-6 will need to understand the "coming to life" that was *denied* to "the rest of the dead" in 20:5 as the same "coming to life" that was *affirmed* in the case of the slain saints in 20:4. But amillennial interpreters—whatever non-literal sense they give to the "coming to life" of v. 4

[4] Daniel 7, which chapter John very clearly alludes to in Rev. 20:4, narrates the rise, the victorious three-and-a-half-year deadly persecuting career of, and the fiery destruction of the fourth "beast" (Dan. 7:7-12, 21, 25), followed, in the same divine judgment scene, by the appearance of "one like a son of man" and the vindication and reign of those upon whom the beast had made deadly war (Dan. 7:9-15, 22, 26-27). In Revelation 13, 17, and 19, John has described a "beast" whose victorious deadly persecuting career also lasts three-and-a-half years, and whose appearance, characteristics, persecuting activity, and fiery destruction all strongly resonate with the fourth beast of Daniel 7 (and its "little horn," Dan. 7:7-8, 20-25). When John sees Jesus (whom he has described as "one like a son of man" in Rev. 1:13 and probably also in 14:14—cf. the connecting use of "clouds" in Rev. 1:7 and Dan. 7:13) appear and conquer the "beast," subjecting him to a fiery destruction in Rev. 19:11-21, John expects his readers to know immediately that he is seeing the Parousia of God and Christ, which they already understand to be the moment of resurrection, reward, and reign for Christians.

[5] E.g. M.G. Kline, "The First Resurrection," *WTJ* 37 (1975), 366-75; G.K. Beale, *The Book of Revelation: A Commentary on the Greek Text* (Grand Rapids: Eerdmans, Carlisle: Paternoster Press, 1999), 149, 998, 1003-1007.

[6] John uses ἔζησαν with the ingressive aorist sense "came to life," but he also allows for a second meaning in line with the normal aorist sense "they lived." This surplus sense allows him to refer to all those who (οἵτινες) had not worshiped the beast or accepted his mark on their hands or foreheads—whether or not the beast managed to kill them.

and the "first resurrection" of v. 5—cannot affirm that what is granted to the faithful in v. 4 will in turn be granted to the rest of the dead at the end of the thousand years. Amillennialists (along with postmillennialists) see the Parousia of God and Christ as happening at the end of the thousand years, and they associate a (literal) general resurrection with the Parousia. Accordingly, they view Rev. 20:11-15 as a vision of a general resurrection and judgment of all humanity that attends the Parousia—which includes those blessed and holy ones who, on their reading, were metaphorically (but not literally) resurrected at the beginning of, or throughout, the thousand years. Since the blessed ones who live and reign with Christ for the thousand years will eventually experience literal resurrection along with everyone else, that which distinguishes them from the rest of humanity is their special, *metaphorical*, resurrection—which the rest of humanity *has not shared, and will never share.*[7] Thus the logical and semantic coherence of the passage breaks down. On one hand John seems obviously to be saying that the partakers of the "first" resurrection experience something *at the beginning of* (or, just conceivably, throughout[8]) the thousand years that will only be experienced by "the rest of the dead" *when the thousand years are completed.* But amillennialists' interpretation of the "first resurrection" as a non-literal spiritual blessing for the faithful witnesses during this age requires them to take away from the "rest of the dead" that which John has just finished promising them.[9]

[7] One might theoretically be able to escape this problem by affirming universal salvation, but that move would be regarded as heterodox by the great majority of amillennialists.

[8] There is actually nothing at all in John's description (20:4, 6) that encourages the idea that the "first resurrection" is anything other than a single event. The partakers all reign with Christ τὰ χίλια ἔτη, "the thousand years."

[9] Kline ("First Resurrection," 366-70) carefully cherry-picks a small handful of the 100 or so New Testament passages in which the very ordinary adjective πρῶτος ("first," as in "first resurrection") can be made to look as though there is something connotative of temporariness and obsolescence inherent to the word (Rev. 21:1, talking about the "first" heaven and earth; 1 Cor. 15:45, 47, talking about the "first Adam"; Heb. 8–9 *passim* talking about the first covenant and tabernacle). He even asks us to accept *an instance that does not exist*, the "first death," which he calls "an expression *virtually* contained in [Rev. 21] verse 4" (my italics). There are, however, dozens of uses of πρῶτος

Second Problem: The Imprisonment and Release of Satan—A Fatal Dilemma

In general, amillennial interpreters assume temporal overlap between the thousand years of Rev. 20:1-10 and the current pre-Parousia age. Given the fact that one of the key characteristics of the thousand years is the binding of Satan and his imprisonment in the abyss (Rev. 20:1-3), they need to find a way to affirm that Satan is *currently* bound and imprisoned, despite the fact that he is plainly understood to be at liberty and to be present and active in the sphere of human affairs not only in Revelation itself, but also in many New Testament texts.[10] In other words, it appears that in trying to relieve one kind of potential disharmony between Revelation and the rest of the New Testament, they are forced to generate another. The standard way of attempting to remedy this new disharmony is to focus in tightly on two things that John says: (1) the reason for Satan's imprisonment was "so that he would not deceive the nations anymore" (v. 3), and (2) when Satan is released, he's going to "come out to deceive the nations…to gather them together for battle" against the saints (v. 8). Thus the usual amillennial proposal is that there is only a narrow and restricted sense in which Satan is bound in the current age: he is bound in the rather narrow sense that he is unable to deceive the nations so as to gather them to prosecute an all-out war on the saints.[11]

in the New Testament in which—as it usually does—it simply means first in temporal order or sequence, without any such connotation (e.g. Mt. 12:45; 20:8, 10; 21:28, 31; 21:36 [pl.], 22:5; 26:17; 27:64; Mk 12:20; 14:12; Lk. 11:26; 14:18; 16:5; 19:16; 20:29; Jn 1:30; Acts 1:1; 20:18; 26:23; 1 Cor. 14:30; Phil. 1:5; 1 Tim. 2:13; 5:12; 2 Tim. 2:6; 4:16; Rev. 1:11, 17; 2:4; 2:5 [pl.]; 4:1), and there are even a goodly number (including and especially in Revelation itself) in which πρῶτος describes something or someone of a better, more substantial, or more permanent nature than that with which the πρῶτος is being contrasted (e.g. Jn 1:30; Acts 26:23; 1 Tim. 5:12; Rev. 1:11, 17; 2:4, 5 [pl.], 8; 22:13).

[10] E.g. Acts 5:3; 1 Cor. 5:5; 2 Cor. 4:3, 4; 11:14; Eph. 6:10-12; 1 Thess. 2:18; 2 Tim. 2:26; 1 Pet. 5:8; 1 John 4:4; 5:19; Rev. 2:10, 13; 12:9-18.

[11] They also often mention Satan's inability to stop the gospel from progressing throughout the world and his inability to hold people captive through demonic forces (cf. Mt. 12:29; Mk 3:27; Lk. 11:21-22). It's not obvious to me, however, as I look at how Jesus uses this parable, that Jesus is

As we will now see, this interpretive move leads to a dilemma each of whose horns contains an irremediable contradiction.

First Horn: The Battle of Rev. 20:7-10 is a Vision of the Beast's Career in Attacking the Church

Let us suppose that we associate Satan's coming up out of the abyss in Rev. 20:7 with the beast's coming up out of the sea in Rev. 12:8–13:1.[12] This would be natural on first look, since according to this view Satan is currently imprisoned in the abyss, and according to Revelation 13 the most salient characteristic of the beast's career (which presumably begins when he "comes up out of the abyss," 11:7; 17:8) will be that he prosecutes an aggressive war on the saints.[13] But herein lies a fatal contradiction. Rev. 20:4 says that it was especially those martyred by the beast who rose and reigned for the thousand years. How can that be, if the beast is not to come on the scene until after the thousand years are over? How can those whom the beast has slain rise victorious from death and reign *before he ever arises to kill them*? This interpretive option absolutely will not work.

Second Horn: The Battle of Rev. 20:7-10 is Not a Vision of the Beast's Career as a Whole, But Only of the Battle of Harmagedon

According to this alternative interpretive option, the beast's career mystically corresponds to the whole age of the church. Throughout this age, the martyrs live and die as witnesses to Christ, and are then welcomed as victors into heaven, where they reign resurrected with Christ. Their resurrection, like the beast's career, is mystical and symbolic rather than literal. This interpretation, having escaped the fatal contradiction of the first horn above, itself runs into an equally fatal contradiction. I will need to back up a bit to explain why this is so.

talking about the devil, as distinct from the demons whom he is overpowering and binding when he does an exorcism.

[12] So Beale, *Revelation*, 987.

[13] See esp. 13:7, 15.

You will recall that amillennialists see "the church age" (i.e. the current age that precedes the Parousia) as the thousand years. In their scheme, the imprisonment of Satan, narrated in Rev. 20:1-3, takes place at the beginning of this age, and Satan remains symbolically imprisoned throughout this age. As mentioned above, in order to hold this interpretation of Rev. 20:1-3 and also escape a glaring contradiction with New Testament (and Book of Revelation) teachings that Satan is now active in deceiving people and persecuting Christians, amillennialists agree in restricting the reference of Satan's binding and imprisonment to a very specific kind of deceptive activity: that deceptive activity by which he gathers the nations to make war on the camp of the saints (cf. the words "deceive" and "nations" in Rev. 20:3, 8).

When we are introduced to the beast in Revelation 13, we find that his brief career as Satan's agent begins in earnest when he rises from the abyss, convinces "the whole earth" (13:3-4) to worship him and his hidden master Satan, and proceeds "to make war on the saints and to conquer them" (13:7; cf. Dan. 7:21-22). With the authority and power of Satan, the beast and his spokesman the false prophet convince all the nations to follow the beast, and they deceive the inhabitants of the earth into making an image of the beast that all worship (Rev. 13:8).[14] The beast's worldwide administration (which encompasses "every tribe, people, language, and *nation*; all inhabitants of the earth," 13:7-8) institutes legal and economic mechanisms by which everyone, on pain of death, is required to worship him (13:14-17). We are given, in other words, every reason to imagine that the career of the beast is the very opposite of a time of Satan's binding and imprisonment as regards his desire to deceive the nations for the purpose of recruiting them to make war against the "camp of the saints" (cf. 20:9).[15] On the contrary, John presents the beast's career as the period not only of Satan's greatest

[14] This is obviously with the exception of Christians, who must be prepared to pay for their non-allegiance with their lives (Rev. 12:9-11; 13:9-10).
[15] See Mealy, *After the Thousand Years* (see p. 10 nt. 1 above), 20 n. 5: "The expression 'camp of the saints' is intentionally used here in the very sense that one would presumably have to give it, given the amillennial interpretation under criticism. That is, if one takes 'the camp of the saints' in Rev. 20:9 as a reference to the church militant on earth prior to the Parousia, as opposed to

and last *deception* of all the nations of the world, but also the period of Satan's greatest and last success in *enlisting the whole world to make war on the saints*. This constitutes a radical, fatal contradiction.

Allow me to summarize this dilemma so that it is absolutely clear. Jesus, Paul, and John, author of Revelation, are all intimately familiar with the complete world transformation that Daniel sees in his vision of the four beasts and the Son of Man (cf. Dan. 7; Mt. 24:1-31; Mk 13:1-27; 2 Thess. 1:5–2:12; Rev. 1:7, 13; 11:7; 12:17; 13:1-8; 17:3, 8-14; 20:4; 22:5). They all identify this total world transition as the Parousia of Jesus Christ, which will bring the career of Daniel's fourth beast and its murderous "little horn" (Dan. 7:8, 11, 20-27) to a decisive end and usher in the age to come, which they look to in hope as an age of resurrection and rule on earth for the faithful. John underlines the radical nature of this transition by stating that all (unrepentant) human beings were killed in the vision in which he saw Jesus come and destroy the beast (Rev. 19:17-21; cf. Rev. 6:12-17; 11:15-19).

Therefore, if you want to plot the current age onto the thousand years, you must plot the endpoint of the thousand years together with the endpoint of the beast's career. This leads to exactly two choices: (1) identify the beast's career of attacking the saints with the battle against the holy city in Rev. 20:7-10, or (2) identify the beast's career with the entire thousand years, and identify the battle of Harmagedon with the battle of Rev. 20:7-10, which happens *after* the thousand years. Neither of these choices turns out to work at all. On one hand, if you try to plot the beast's career after the end of the thousand years, you make absurd John's statement in Rev. 20:4 that it was those whom the beast had killed who rose and reigned for the thousand years. On the other hand, if you try to plot the beast's career concurrent with the thousand years, you end up with more or less the worst contradiction imaginable within Revelation itself. You're proposing that John described the same period first as the time

the eschatological community of the kingdom following the Parousia (*sc.* the New Jerusalem), then it follows that the most salient feature of the beast's three-and-a-half-year career is that it is that time during which he prosecutes an all-out war on 'the camp of the saints' (cf. 12:6, 13-17; 13:5-7)."

of Satan's last, greatest, and most completely successful deception of unrepentant humanity for the purposes of attacking and destroying the saints who follow Jesus (Rev. 12:17–13:17), and then as the time during which Satan, having been bound with a great chain and thrown into the prison of the abyss, sat locked in and sealed there, powerless to deceive the nations so as to get them to attack the saints (Rev. 20:1-3, 7).

Third Problem: Expulsion from Heaven to Earth, or Capture and Imprisonment in the Abyss?

This, as I mentioned above, is an independent problem, and I will demonstrate that it is independently fatal to amillennialism.

As we have seen, the amillennial model requires the thousand years to be plotted so that it ends concurrently with the end of the career of the beast. The very same principles of recapitulative plotting also require that the fall of Satan from heaven (Rev. 12), which begins his association with the pseudo-resurrected beast (12:17–13:1), be identified with the imprisonment of Satan in the abyss in Rev. 20:1-2. For example, G.K. Beale says,

> The parallels between chs. 12 and 20, though the chapters are not identical at every point, suggest that they depict the same events and mutually interpret one another.[16]

Beale proceeds to lay out a table of seven proposed parallels which we will now examine.[17]

(1) The scenes of Rev. 12.7-11 and 20:1-3 are both asserted to be "heavenly." This is incorrect. In 12:7 John sees a war in heaven; in 20:1 John, having just witnessed the battle of Harmagedon on earth, sees an angel "coming down out of heaven with the key of the abyss in his hand," after which—in the realm beneath heaven—he captures the devil and imprisons him in the abyss. Nothing in 20:1-3 happens in heaven. The mere mention

[16] Beale, *Revelation*, 992.

[17] All seven proposed parallels are listed in Beale, *Revelation*, 992.

of heaven as the origin of the constabulary angel does not qualify the scene as "heavenly."

(2) The "angelic battle" of Rev. 12:9 is made parallel to a "presumed angelic battle" in 20:2. There is no textual basis to presume that the angel and/or other angels must battle with Satan in 20:2 in order to capture him, given that no battle is described in the scene of 19:17-21. The beast and his armies may have battle in mind, but they are summarily captured and/or slain. Parallels that only appear when you add things to the text are not parallels.

(3) "Satan cast to earth" (12:9) is offered as a parallel to "Satan cast into the abyss" (20:3). This isn't a parallel. Revelation's cosmology is consistent. The earth is never conflated with the abyss.

(4) The devil is called "the great dragon, the ancient serpent, the one called the devil and Satan, the one deceiving the whole inhabited earth" in 12:9, and he is called "the great dragon, the ancient serpent, who is the devil and Satan" in 20:2. There is, of course, no dispute as to the fact that the devil is a major character in both scenes. John's resumption of the same names and descriptors is a familiar technique that he uses to make his readers aware that he is reintroducing a character. Beale notes that in Rev. 12:9 the devil is said to be the deceiver of the whole inhabited earth, whereas in 20:3 he is said to be imprisoned so that he will be restrained from deceiving the nations any longer. These two items do not match. In fact, the readers will remember that very soon after being hurled to the earth in Rev. 12:9, the deceiver recruited the beast, and through the beast created his greatest deception ever—successfully getting all of faithless humanity not only to worship the beast and thereby worship himself (12:17–13:4), but also to see the faithful as enemies and to attack and kill them. This is the deception[18] that the readers will have in mind when they hear that the devil is going to be prevented from deceiving the nations "any longer" in Rev. 20:3. When read contextually, this is an anti-parallel.

[18] Along with the deception of the false miracles and the demonic influence that the devil produced in order to gather the faithless nations to the battle of Harmagedon (16:12-16).

(5) "Satan's expression of 'great wrath because he knows he has little time'" (12:12b) is put in parallel with "Satan to be 'released for a short time' after his imprisonment" (20:3). To begin with, these two expressions for a short time are not the same. In 12:12 it is ὀλίγον χαιρόν and it is μίκρον χρόνον in 20:3. Secondly, in order for there to be a parallel, the condition following the casting to earth ought to correspond to the imprisonment in the abyss, not to whatever happens after that imprisonment is over. This is neither a verbal nor a narrative-level parallel.

(6) "Satan's fall, resulting in the kingdom of Christ (v. 10) and his saints (v. 11; note the 'conquering' theme)" is put alongside "Satan's fall, resulting in the kingdom of Christ and his saints (v. 4)." This is the first proposed parallel that has some substance. It is weakened, however, by the fact that 12:10-11 is naturally read as proleptic—just as is the nearby announcement of God's reign in 11:15-17. God has begun to reign while the nations still "rage" (ὀργίζω, 11:18). The devil himself, when cast to the earth, also "rages" (also ὀργίζω, 12:17), and through the beast he gets the nations to rage against the holy ones, the brothers and sisters, murdering them on a global scale (cf. 12:11, 17; 13:7, 15). The holy ones, however, are on the winning side. They "overcame" the devil in the fight for the kingdom by dying for their faith (12:11). The faithful join God and Jesus Christ in the battle to re-take the earth from sinful angels and humans, and this battle is not to be identified with the reign that takes place when the beast and the rebel nations have been ousted and the realm has been secured (cf. Dan. 7:11-14, 18, 21, 25-27; Rev. 19:19–20:6). It is *after* the fight with the raging devil and the raging nations, *after* they have been slain by the beast, that the conquerors rise and reign (20:4).

(7) Beale says that in both 12:11 and 20:4 the saints' "kingship" is based not only on the fall of Satan and Christ's victory, but also on their faithfulness even to death. This parallel appears contrived because (a) there is no mention of the saints' "kingship" in 12:11, but rather victory in battle, and (b) there is no mention of a "fall" of Satan in 20:1-3.

Let us now see how this business of looking at potential parallels works out when we do not treat the identity between

Rev. 12:1-17 and 20:1-3 as a foregone conclusion. Consider the following bias-neutral table of comparative characteristics for the two scenes.

	Revelation 12:1-17	Revelation 20:1-3
Who	The devil, Michael and his angels.	The devil, an angel from heaven.
What	A battle and defeat of Satan. Expulsion from heaven to earth.	A capture, chaining, and imprisonment of Satan in the abyss.
Where	In heaven, then on earth.	Under heaven ("I saw an angel coming down from heaven with a chain," 20:1), then under the earth (in the abyss, v. 3).
When	"A short time" (12:12) before the Parousia of Christ, which appears to be the 3½ year period referred to in 12:6, 14; 13:5.	"A thousand years" before the battle of 20:7-10.
Why	Satan appears to be expelled so that he will not be able to accuse the saints any longer (12:10), or because he has rebelled in heaven (12:7-8).	So that he will no longer be able to deceive the nations (20:3).
Results	Satan sets off on a brief and intense rampage against the saints on earth (12:12-17).	Satan sits in chains in the abyss for a thousand years (20:3).

If we confine ourselves to what the text actually says, the only thing that is the same between these two passages is Satan's involvement in each scene. And that makes perfect sense because the two passages narrate the first two of three *successive stages* in the story of his ultimate defeat:

- Satan is first expelled from heaven, after which he runs rampant on earth, using the beast and the false prophet to deceive the nations into worshiping him and into killing those who worship God and serve Jesus (Rev. 12–13).
- Satan's association with the beast and false prophet is broken when those two are defeated, captured, and destroyed by Christ at the battle of Harmagedon (Rev. 16:13-17; 19:17-21). Satan himself is then captured as well, and is expelled from the earth and imprisoned in the abyss (Rev. 20:1-3).
- A thousand years later he is released from the abyss, but he immediately reverts to his old crime of deceiving the unrepentant into attacking the faithful (Rev. 20:7-10).

This narrative sequence is clear, meaningful, and coherent. There is no plausible way to assert that an unprejudiced reader could turn aside from this coherent storyline, and instead equate two episodes (Rev. 12:7–13:1 and Rev. 20:1-3) that are narrated with markedly different, seemingly incompatible, and independently meaningful characterizations of the "what," "where," "when," "why," and "results" of each episode. In other words, the two narrations differ significantly and meaningfully in terms of *every one* of the elements that could potentially have signaled John's readers that they were now, in Rev. 20:1-3, seeing an additional viewpoint on something they had already seen in Revelation 12. John is entirely capable of accomplishing the kind of identification and recapitulation that Beale and others claim to see going on here, and it is possible to demonstrate in detail how John achieves it.[19] It is clear, however, that an unbiased reader—especially a sequential reader—could never conclude from the actual verbal data of the two passages that the events of Rev. 12:7–13:1 and Rev. 20:1-3 are intended to be taken as identical. Given that an amillennial reading of

[19] For a detailed demonstration of this, see Mealy, *After the Thousand Years* (see p. 10 nt. 1 above), 13-14, 59-94, and *passim* chs. 5–9.

Rev. 20:1-10 *requires* this identification, the impossibility of it amounts to a fatal problem for the amillennial reading.[20]

These three problems of amillennialism, the one serious and the other two independently fatal, show that amillennialism absolutely will not work as an interpretive approach to Revelation 20. Let us step back for just a moment and remind ourselves why amillennial interpreters go to such lengths to try to map the thousand years of Rev. 20:1-10 onto the current age. In a word, their motivation is one of *harmonization.* In the first place, they observe that Jesus, Paul, and Peter agree in looking ahead to the renewal, the re-creation, of the whole world at the Parousia of Jesus. But we've seen in Chapters 1 and 2 that John's narration of Revelation 19–21 makes good and satisfying sense when the binding and underworld imprisonment of the devil, the resurrection of the saints, and the new creation are *all* understood to happen at the Parousia, so this is an illusory problem. Secondly, they observe that the wedding of Christ and the church, the community of the faithful, logically and theologically belongs at the Parousia of Jesus. As in the case of the timing of the new creation, we've seen in Chapters 1 and 2 that the wedding of Christ the King and his bride, the church *and* the inauguration thousand years happens at the Parousia, so this too is an illusory problem. Thirdly, they do not see evidence anywhere else in the New Testament for the idea of an age that begins with the Parousia of Jesus and is characterized by resurrection for the faithful only—and refusal of resurrection to the unrepentant. I admit that *if* there were no such New Testament evidence external to the Book of Revelation, this would present a puzzle for interpreters who believe that all Scripture is inspired by the same God and that therefore all passages ought ultimately to be capable of mutual harmonization. But given that the amillennial solution to this problem is fraught with such insuperable difficulties, it is rather puzzling that so few interpreters choose an alternative option that has been on the table for well over a century now—that of reading Rev. 20:1-6 a-temporally.

The a-temporal approach concedes that on the surface narrative level, Rev. 20:1-10 pictures events that begin with Christ's

[20] I make this argument in my article, "Revelation is One" (see p. 10 nt. 1), 131-53 (151).

coming in glory, but it goes on to suggest that the millennium is best taken as a purely symbolic picture of a special reward for the slain martyrs. This avoids the fatal problems of both historic premillennialism and amillennialism, but in my view it has a major drawback. In Revelation, from the beginning, every reader is given the sense that to be a follower of Jesus Christ is to face persecution and the danger of losing one's mortal life. *Every believer* is a martyr (μάρτυς, one who testifies to Christ), and *everyone* is expected to continue testifying to the point of laying down their life. Most a-temporal interpreters present the millennial reign in a way that undermines this crucial pastoral thrust by assuming that John pictures the millennium as being reserved for an elite class of martyrs. In my view that is its most significant weakness. Nonetheless, for those who for one reason or another fail to be persuaded of the new creation millennialism reading presented in this book, I respectfully recommend exploration in the direction of a-temporal approaches.[21]

In Chapter 4 I will demonstrate that a clear solution exists to the only significant harmonization problem that now appears to remain between a premillennial reading of Revelation 20 and the rest of the NT. The picture in Rev. 20:4-6 of a resurrection for the faithful alone at Jesus Christ's Parousia can in fact be shown to have multiple parallels in the teachings of Jesus and Paul, as well as the key resurrection oracle of the prophet Isaiah.

[21] For a-temporal interpretations prior to 1992, see Mealy, *After the Thousand Years* (see p. 10 nt. 1 above), 29-46. For essentially a-temporal approaches in English post 1992, see e.g. R. Bauckham, *The Theology of the Book of Revelation* (New Testament Theology; Cambridge, UK: Cambridge University Press, 1993); G.D. Fee, *Revelation: A New Covenant Commentary* (Eugene, OR: Cascade Books, 2011); M.J. Gorman, *Reading Revelation Responsibly: Uncivil Worship and Witness: Following the Lamb into the New Creation* (Eugene, OR: Cascade Books, 2011), 144-45; C.R. Koester, *Revelation: A New Translation with Introduction and Commentary* (Anchor Yale Bible, 38A; New Haven: Yale University Press, 2014); M. Maxwell, *Revelation* (Doubleday Bible Commentary; New York: Doubleday, 1998); R.J. McKelvey, *The Millennium and the Book of Revelation* (Cambridge, UK: Lutterworth, 1999); M.G. Reddish, *Revelation* (Smyth & Helwys Bible Commentary; Macon, GA: Smyth & Helwys, 2001); J.L. Resseguie, *Revelation: A Narrative Commentary* (Grand Rapids, MI: Baker Academic, 2009); S.P. Woodman, *The Book of Revelation* (SCM Core Text; London: SCM Press, 2008).

Chapter 4
Selective Resurrection in the New Testament: Rebutting the Main Amillennial Critique of Premillennialism

Jesus on "The Resurrection from among the Dead"

In my view, the alleged problem of the disharmony between Rev. 20:4-6 and the rest of the New Testament (if these verses are understood to speak of a selective resurrection for the faithful alone) disappears when we understand the implications of the expression "the resurrection from among the dead" (Gr. ἡ ἀνάσατσις [ἡ] ἐκ [τῶν] νεκρῶν).

Let us start with Jesus. In responding to a skeptical question about resurrection from the Sadducees, Jesus says,

Lk. 20:35

> 35 ...but those who are considered worthy of a place in that age and in the resurrection from the dead neither marry nor are given in marriage.

"That age" is a standard first-century Jewish expression for the age of God's Kingdom on earth that follows the current age. Jesus is saying that there is going to be a judgment of all the dead at the transition point between this age and the age to come. The result of that judgment will be that some of the dead will be found worthy of participation in the age to come, which implies that the rest of the dead will be found *unworthy.* Those found worthy will be resurrected "from the dead" (ἐκ νεκρῶν), which plainly implies that the rest of the dead *will remain dead.*

This will be a novel idea to many, who, reading their English Bibles, have always assumed that the phrase "from the dead" means "from the state of death." It does not. The word translated as "the dead" in this expression is *plural*, and refers to the dead people—that is, all of those who have died.[1] Thus Jesus says a little later in v. 38, "[God] is not the God of the dead (θεὸς δὲ οὐκ ἔστιν νεκρῶν), but of the living (ἀλλὰ ζώντων); for to him all of them are alive."

When Jesus says that some of the dead are going to be resurrected *from among* the rest, he is saying that the others *are not* going to be resurrected. They're going to stay dead—at least at that time. What will ultimately happen to those "left behind" in the realm of the dead when those found worthy are raised from among them? Jesus doesn't go into that in this teaching, because the final destiny of those who are found unworthy is not what the argument with the Sadducees is about: it is about whether *anyone* will be resurrected (see Lk. 20:27 || Mt. 22:23 || Mk 12:18).

New Testament authors (and Jesus himself) speak many times about him rising or being raised from among the dead. Conceptually speaking, when Jesus dies, he takes up company with the dead. When he rises on the third day, he leaves the dead and returns to the company of the living. He thus arises from among the dead (ἐκ νεκρῶν), leaving them behind in the realm of the dead. Alternatively, he rises (i.e. stands up again) as a living person, leaving the rest of the dead still lying down in their graves and tombs.[2] The same principle—and precisely the same terminology—applies in the case of Jesus' story of the Rich Man and Lazarus:

[1] The word νεκρῶν ("the dead") is in the genitive case in this expression, which, following the preposition ἐκ ("away from," or "from among"), carries an ablative sense—the worthy dead are going to be separated from among the rest of the larger group of the dead by being resurrected.

[2] The question of whether the realm of the dead is to be imagined concretely, as the realm of graves and tombs, or cosmologically, as the underworld realm of Sheol or Hades or the abyss (as in Rom. 10:7), remains immaterial to the point here.

Lk. 16:31

> 31 He said to him, "If they do not listen to Moses and the prophets, neither will they be convinced even if someone rises from the dead."[3]

This is the punch line of the story. Abraham is refusing the rich man's request to send Lazarus back from among the dead to warn his brothers about the danger of an afterlife of torment. If Lazarus were to "rise from among the dead" to perform this messenger role, he would obviously leave the rest of the dead where they are, in Hades. The same conception lies behind John's way of talking about Jesus' friend Lazarus, whom Jesus "raised from among the dead" (Jn 12:1, 9, 17).[4]

The largely unrecognized fact here is that the concept of resurrection from among the dead is *inherently* exclusive. A Greek speaker simply could not talk about a resurrection of all of the dead as a "resurrection from among the dead," ἀνάσατσις ἐκ [τῶν] νεκρῶν. The burden of proof here lies squarely on the shoulders of those who wish to argue either (1) that ἐκ [τῶν] νεκρῶν connotes something like "from death" or "from the realm of the dead,"[5] or (2) that the distinction indicated by the phrase ἐκ [τῶν] νεκρῶν is somehow a distinction between two outcomes for participants in a single general resurrection (acquittal and life versus condemnation), rather than a distinction between those resurrected and those not resurrected.[6] All such

[3] Gr. οὐδὲ ἐάν τις ἐκ νεκρῶν ἀναστῇ.

[4] In each of these instances the expression ἐκ νεκρῶν is used. I add the word "among" to remind readers that "the dead" is a plural substantive and means the people who are dead.

[5] I have made a search of Christian letters, sermons, treatises, and apocalypses written in Greek up to about 600 CE, and I'm prepared to make the claim that this expression is never employed during that period when (1) a general resurrection or (2) a resurrection to judgment (rather than life) is in view. I also have surveyed the ancient Greek literature contained in the Perseus online database at Tufts University to see how secular authors use the words and phrases ἀνάσατσις, ἀνάσατσις ἐκ (τῶν) νεκρῶν, ἐκ (τῶν) νεκρῶν, ἐκ θανάτου, and related formulations. The more than 200 *secular* Greek works that I have consulted using Perseus do not use the terminology of rising or returning "from the dead" at all.

[6] This approach comes up regularly in conservative Reformed commentaries. For example, see N. Geldenhuys (*Commentary on the Gospel of Luke* [Grand

reasoning reveals itself as special pleading based on the foregone conclusion that the New Testament knows nothing of a selective resurrection at the Parousia that only the faithful enjoy. *But that is exactly the question at issue.* After ruling out a selective-resurrection reading of Rev. 20:4-6 on the basis that the rest of the New Testament supposedly knows of no such thing, interpreters cannot then turn around and refuse to own up to the presence of prima facie evidence elsewhere in the New Testament for selective resurrection on the very same basis.

The words of Isaiah in Isa. 26:13-19 contribute further evidence that Jesus is talking about a selective resurrection in Lk. 20:35.

Isa. 26:13-19

> 13 O LORD our God,
> other lords besides you have ruled over us,
> but we acknowledge your name alone.
> 14 The dead do not live;
> shades do not rise—
> because you have punished and destroyed them,
> and wiped out all memory of them.
> 15 But you have increased the nation, O LORD,
> you have increased the nation; you are glorified;
> you have enlarged all the borders of the land.
> 16 O LORD, in distress they sought you,
> they poured out a prayer
> when your chastening was on them.
> 17 Like a woman with child,
> who writhes and cries out in her pangs
> when she is near her time,
> so were we because of you, O LORD;
> 18 we were with child, we writhed,

Rapids: Eerdmans, 1979], 513-14, nt. 9). Having consulted more than a dozen technical commentaries on the Gospel of Luke by reformed scholars, I have not yet encountered any argument against the view I'm asserting here on the basis of grammatical principles or of demonstrated uses of the terms and phrases in question. The justification is always (if there is any justification at all) that the New Testament doesn't teach selective resurrection, therefore Jesus cannot be teaching selective resurrection in this passage. But this argument is patently circular.

but we gave birth only to wind.
We have won no victories on earth,
and no one is born to inhabit the world.
19 Your dead shall live, their corpses shall rise.[7]
O dwellers in the dust, awake and sing for joy!
For your dew is a radiant dew,
and the earth will give birth to those long dead.[8]

Isaiah here prophesies that the moment of redemption for the persecuted faithful (26:13, 18) will be a moment of resurrection for them (26:19), but not for the dead in general (26:14), who will remain dead, serving out a sentence of punishment and destruction. It is baffling that so many Christian interpreters more or less completely overlook this passage from Isaiah. After all, Jesus and the writers of the New Testament held Isaiah in the highest possible esteem as a divinely-inspired prophet who saw and recorded many dramatic and revelatory visions about the end of this world and the transition to the world to come. They unequivocally regarded his prophecies as important revelations from God about the future that must come to fulfillment.[9] In view of the unique regard in which Jesus and the New Testament authors hold Isaiah, anyone who wishes to rule out the idea of a selective resurrection for the faithful based on a *harmonistic* approach to the Bible as a whole (which, after all, includes Isaiah's prophecies) automatically assumes a dual burden of proof here. They must demonstrate both (1) that Isa. 26:13-19 did not originally refer to a refusal of resurrection to the oppressors and the granting of resurrection to the persecuted faithful, and (2) that Jesus and the writers of the New Testament also did not read Isa. 26:13-19 in that way.

[7] Following Targums, Syriac, and LXX. Heb. has the almost impossible "my corpse, they shall rise."
[8] Lit. "to the shades," Heb. *rephaim*.
[9] NT authors' interest in Isaiah is no less evident in relation to Isaiah 24–27, the so-called "Isaiah Apocalypse," than in the rest of Isaiah. See, e.g., the many references to Isa. 24–27 in the list of OT passages quoted or alluded to in New Testament passages at the back of the UBS Greek New Testament, *Novum Testamentum Graece* (4th edn; Stuttgart: German Bible Society, 1993). Paul even quotes Isa. 26:19 in Eph. 5:14, applying its resurrection language metaphorically (as he often does) to the radically new life of Christians.

Luke's Gospel contains another saying of Jesus that supports the idea of a resurrection that is exclusively for the benefit of the faithful:

Lk. 14:12-14

> 12 He said also to the one who had invited him, "When you give a luncheon or a dinner, do not invite your friends or your brothers or your relatives or rich neighbors, in case they may invite you in return, and you would be repaid. 13 But when you give a banquet, invite the poor, the crippled, the lame, and the blind. 14 And you will be blessed, because they cannot repay you, for you will be repaid at the resurrection of the righteous."

The most natural sense of these words is that a resurrection is coming in which the righteous—and they alone—will take part. Such an exclusive sense links perfectly with what Jesus says in Lk. 20:35 above. Obviously the wording of Luke 14:12-14 is not strictly incompatible with the concept of a general resurrection that has two qualitative outcomes—one for the just and one for the unjust. But if there is a burden of proof in relation to this saying, it lies with the person who wishes to argue that Jesus is talking about a general resurrection rather than a selective one.

Since we've now seen that there is good evidence in the teachings of Jesus for the idea of selective resurrection at the transition to the age to come, let us turn now to see what evidence we can find from elsewhere in the New Testament for this concept.

Paul on the Resurrection Hope of Believers

To begin with, we can note that the apostle Paul uses the terminology of "resurrection from among the dead" when he expresses the hope that he personally will experience resurrection to eternal life:

Phil. 3:10-11

> 10 I want to know Christ and the power of his resurrection and the sharing of his sufferings by becoming like him in

> his death, 11 if somehow I may attain the resurrection from the dead.

I am going to assume for the purposes of this study that Paul believed that all of the dead would be resurrected at some point.[10] But Paul hopes for far more than resurrection as such—which he believes awaits all human beings, the evil and the good, the lost and the saved. Paul wants to belong to Jesus and to experience resurrection life at his side when he comes again to reign in glory (e.g. Rom. 6:8; 8:17-23; 1 Cor. 15:22-23, 52; Phil. 3:20-21; Col. 3:4; 1 Thess. 4:15-17; 2 Tim. 2:10-13). The NRSV version of Phil. 3:10 quoted above actually under-translates Paul's words as "the resurrection from the dead," but Paul is more expressive, referring to "the out-resurrection from among the dead" (ἡ ἐξανάστασις ἡ ἐκ νεκρῶν). The fact that he speaks this way to express this personal hope stands as strong prima facie evidence that he *did not expect* the resurrection of all of the dead to occur when Jesus comes again. His teaching in 1 Corinthians 15 coheres with this:

1 Cor. 15:12, 20-24

> 12 Now if Christ is proclaimed as raised from the dead, how can some of you say there is no resurrection of the dead? … 20 But in fact Christ has been raised from the dead, the first fruits of those who have died. 21 For since death came through a human being, the resurrection of the dead has also come through a human being; 22 for as all die in Adam, so all will be made alive in Christ. 23 But each in his own order: Christ the first fruits, then at his coming those who belong to Christ. 24 Then comes the end [or "then the rest"], when he hands over the kingdom to God the Father, after he has destroyed every ruler and every authority and power.

Paul is not trying in this passage to give the Corinthians an exhaustive teaching about the end of the world. Like Jesus in Lk. 14:12-14 and 20:35, his focus here is specifically responsive to the context of the discussion—which concerns the

[10] Although Paul never writes anything specific about the resurrection of the unrepentant, Acts quotes him as affirming belief in it (Acts 24:15).

resurrection hope of believers. Consonant with his way of talking about his own resurrection hope in Phil. 3:10-11, Paul says here that the resurrection of believers at Christ's coming in glory constitutes the second of three major divisions[11] that together make up the resurrection of all humanity. Christ by himself comprises the first division, and he rises early, like the firstfruits offering before the main harvest.[12] Then comes the division of those who belong to him, who correspond under this metaphor to the main harvest, who rise when he comes again. Then presumably comes the final group, unrepentant humanity, which would correspond to the final post-harvest stage of gathering and burning of the weeds, the chaff, and the stubble.[13] Paul pulls back from full explicitness at this point and simply calls the last stage "the end" (τὸ τέλος). This may be (1) because he finds himself uneasy at referring to the resurrection of those who do not "belong to Christ" as their being "made alive in Christ" (see 15:22; Paul doesn't want to leave the possible impression of universal salvation to incorruptible life), or (2) because he wishes to keep the focus on the faithful, or (3) because he doesn't have clear revelation about how the final resurrection and judgment of the unrepentant will turn out.

There may also be a second metaphor at play here if—as seems possible—the military connotation of τάγμα is consciously in his mind. Paul may be thinking of a military parade, in which divisions of soldiers march forward one after the other. That

[11]The word I'm rendering as "division" is τάγμα, which occurs only here in the Greek New Testament. It usually carries a non-technical sense of a portion of a larger group like an army. See e.g. Diodorus Siculus, *Library*, 13.109, in which it refers to three ad hoc sections into which Dionysius of Syracuse divided his infantry for the purposes of attacking the city of Carthage.

[12] Cf. Lev. 23:9-14; Deut. 26:1-11.

[13] See Mt. 3:11-12 || Lk. 3:16-17; cf. also Mt. 13:30, in which weeds are bundled in the field for later burning along with the stubble of the wheat. For the agricultural practice of burning stubble after the harvest as a metaphor for the destruction of the wicked, see Exod. 15:7; Isa. 5:24; 27:4; 33:11 (in this verse stubble and chaff are associated); 47:14; Obad. 1:18; Nah. 1:10; Mal. 4:1. Joel 2:3-5 pictures a marauding army as a stubble-clearing fire that devours the whole surface of the land as it advances, leaving nothing alive in its wake.

would explain the sense of sequence that is created by the phraseology, "Christ…then those who belong to him…then[14] the end" (or, "then the last division"[15]).

Where did Paul get the concept of a future resurrection of humanity that is divided between the faithful (those who "belong to Jesus") and the rest of humanity? Clearly he could have gotten it from Jesus on the basis of familiarity with sayings such as those that Luke quotes in Lk. 14:12-14 and 20:35. It is equally possible that in addition to this his thinking was formed by Isa. 26:14, 19. After all, Paul is an avid student of Isaiah's prophecies, and in one passage he even cites Isa. 26:19, the very passage in which Isaiah prophesies resurrection for the faithful and denial of resurrection to the oppressors:

Eph. 5:14

> 14 Sleeper, awake!
> Rise from the dead,[16]
> and Christ will shine on you.

It is true that Paul here applies the resurrection hope in Isaiah metaphorically to the new life of Christians in this age. But this does not in the least reduce the probability that he understood Isa. 26:19 as a prophecy of resurrection for the faithful at the transition to the age to come—and denial of resurrection to their

[14] No significance attaches to Paul's use of the synonyms εἶτα and ἔπειτα here, the choice of which simply depends on considerations of euphony (i.e. what sounds better). It is very ordinary for authors to change up or alternate the use of these two words in expressing a chronological sequence, so as to avoid dull repetition. Which word is used in each place simply depends on what makes the sentence sound the smoothest. Neither of these two words, moreover, implies immediate chronological succession, as could be over-interpreted from the English word "then," which translates them both. Christ's resurrection is not immediately followed by the resurrection of believers, and by the same token, the resurrection of the rest of humanity does not necessarily follow immediately upon the resurrection of believers. It simply happens afterwards.

[15] "The final division" would be the meaning of τὸ τέλος if the military metaphor of "every person within his own division" (τάγμα) is (still) active. See BAGD, τάγμα (1) (a)(b) and τέλος (4), and the references in those two entries. In the Greek version of his *Tactics*, Η ΤΑΚΤΙΚΗ, Arrian appears to speak of the army proceeding "division by division," τάγμα τάγματι (28:2).

[16] Quoting Isa. 26:19; cf. also Isa. 51:17; 52:1; 60:1.

persecutors at that time. After all, Paul applies the hope of future (literal, bodily) resurrection metaphorically to the living of a renewed Christian life in many places in his letters, including multiple times in Ephesians itself (Rom. 6:4-5, 13; 7:6; 2 Cor. 5:17; Eph. 2:5-6; 4:22-24; 5:14; Col. 2:12-13; 3:1-3).

Let us look at one more passage in Paul's letters that bears on the question of Paul's view of resurrection: 1 Thess. 4:13-17. First let me supply some background.

Paul founded a community of Christians in Thessalonica on his second missionary journey in 49 CE (see Acts 17:1-9). The core community of those originally converted by his preaching was made up of Jews and God-fearing Gentiles. The God-fearers subscribed to the monotheistic faith of Judaism but were not circumcised. Paul, because of heavy persecution, was only able to stay with the new believers a few weeks, so their default ideas about the future of the world, if Paul did not expressly teach them differently, would have been Jewish. With the exception of the skeptical ruling-class Sadducees, first-century Jews generally shared the hope of resurrection. There were, however, two main competing views as to when the resurrection of the faithful would occur. One view was that they would take part in a single, universal resurrection of all humanity for judgment at the very end of the world. In it, every person who had ever lived would have to give an account to God for how they had lived. This resurrection would take place after the glorious worldwide kingdom of Messiah, the last age of this world. Some Jewish literature contemporary with the New Testament gives expression to this view.[17] The other view was that those who were faithful to God throughout history would rise to take part in Messiah's kingdom on earth.[18] The rabbis were divided, with perhaps the majority siding with the latter view.[19] As we've seen above, Jesus and Paul both express themselves in a

[17] See, e.g., *4 Ezra* 7:26-43; 8:52-54; *Apocalypse of Baruch* (= *2 Baruch*) 29–30; *Life of Adam and Eve* 29:7-10; 48:1-3; 51:1-2. All of these works appear to expect a general resurrection to occur *after* the hoped-for golden age or messianic age.

[18] See *Genesis Rabba* 96.

[19] See M. Greenberg, D. Boyarin, and S. Siegel, "Resurrection," in *Encyclopaedia Judaica*, vol. 17 (ed. M. Berenbaum and F. Skolnik; 2nd edn; Detroit: Macmillan Reference USA, 2007), 240-44.

way that aligns them with the latter view. But Paul, in the short time he got to spend with his new Thessalonian believers, may not have found a chance to talk in any depth about this subject. And even if he did, disputes or questions could easily have arisen later. Paul's original converts could have remained less than fully clear on the subject, or Jews who converted to Jesus after Paul's departure could have brought with them the general resurrection concept, resulting in confusion or uncertainty. In any case, it is evident that the community had asked Paul for clarification as to whether or not the resurrection of believers would attend the glorious Parousia of Jesus as Messiah. In response to this and other issues and questions, Paul wrote his first letter to the Thessalonian believers around 50 CE, a year after the founding of their Christian community.

1 Thess. 4:13-17

> 13 But we do not want you to be uninformed, brothers and sisters, about those who have died,[20] so that you may not grieve as others do who have no hope. 14 For since we believe that Jesus died and rose again, even so, through Jesus, God will bring with him those who have died.[21] 15 For this we declare to you by the word of the Lord,[22] that we who are alive, who are left until the coming of the Lord, will by no means precede those who have died.[23] 16 For the Lord himself, with a cry of command, with the archangel's call and with the sound of God's trumpet, will descend from heaven, and the dead in Christ will rise first. 17 Then we who are alive, who are left, will be caught up in the clouds together with them to meet the Lord in the air; and so we will be with the Lord forever.

There is one thing Paul is certainly *not* doing here, and that is reassuring the believers that there is such a thing as bodily resurrection for Christians. In a community whose core was

[20] Lit. "And we don't want you to be ignorant about those who are asleep." "Those who are asleep" is a common euphemism for people who've died.

[21] Lit. "fallen asleep."

[22] See Mt. 24:30-31; Mk 13:26-27.

[23] Lit. "fallen asleep."

Jewish and which had received its instruction in the faith by Paul, belief in bodily resurrection for the faithful would have been an absolute given. If skepticism about resurrection as such had been the problem behind 1 Thessalonians, Paul would certainly have lambasted them even more thoroughly than he did the (mostly Greek) Corinthians a few years later (cf. 1 Cor. 15:1-19). *The only issue that could plausibly be up in the air for them was the question of whether the resurrection of believers would precede or follow the coming age of Christ's glorious messianic kingdom.* And this is exactly what Paul zooms in on. He says that he wants them to be clear about what to expect regarding Christians who have died so that they won't "grieve as others do who have no hope" (1 Thess. 4:13). Why, if they believed in resurrection, might some of the Thessalonians still grieve like non-believers with no hope of resurrection? If some of them subscribed to the view that there would be one universal resurrection after the "times of the Messiah," they might well grieve just about as bitterly as others. After all, the first generation of Christians dearly hoped to see the Parousia of Christ in their lifetimes, and they would have expected for Christ's reign to last a whole age—at least several centuries (cf. Isa. 65:17-22). Thus, those who lived to see the Parousia, on the universal resurrection view, would have to wait a whole age to be reunited in resurrection with their loved ones. It is understandable that such people might face intense grief at the thought of this indefinitely long separation, compounded by uncomprehending sorrow at the thought that those who had died had so narrowly missed the blessing of taking part in the glories of Christ's kingdom.

To these people Paul replies: those who have died *will not* be left in their graves for the glorious messianic age when Jesus comes. *We who are left alive will not precede them* into Christ's kingdom (v. 15) when he comes to reign.[24] They will rise *first*, then we will be caught up with them to meet the Lord in the air (vv. 16-17). Paul's double emphasis on the *timing* of the resurrection of the faithful confirms that the issue disturbing the

[24] The phrase ἡ παρουσία τοῦ κυρίου means that Jesus comes in glory to reign as Messiah on earth and nothing less.

Thessalonians was not *whether* resurrection of believers was to be hoped for, but *when* their resurrection would take place.[25]

Modern, doctrinally-minded readers of Paul's letters might find his teachings on eschatology patchy in comparison to what they would have liked him to have written. But we are often reading his letters over the shoulder of first-century people who faced particular disputes or questions, and we are reading responses composed by Paul to address those particular disputes or questions—not to fulfill our desire for a comprehensive doctrinal exposition. It is easier when he is relatively specific as to the mistaken ideas that he is responding to, as in 1 Corinthians 15, but other times, as in 1 Thessalonians 4–5, we must to a certain extent infer the shape of the problematic ideas from the shape of his responses. The interpretation of 1 Thess. 4:13-17 that I have put forward can be accepted with a good level of confidence because it makes sense not only in terms of the historical context of uncertainty within first-century Judaism about the timing of the resurrection, but also in terms of the logic and internal consistency of the passage itself. In addition, reading the passage in the light of this interpretation sheds additional light on Paul's teachings about resurrection in 1 Corinthians:

1 Cor. 15:22-28

> $_{22}$ for as all die in Adam, so all will be made alive in Christ. $_{23}$ But each in his own order: Christ the first fruits, then at his coming those who belong to Christ. $_{24}$ Then comes the end, when he hands over the kingdom to God the Father, after he has destroyed every ruler and every authority and power. $_{25}$ For he must reign until he has put all his enemies under his feet.[26] $_{26}$ The last enemy to be destroyed is death. $_{27}$ But when it says, "All things are put in subjection," it is plain that this does not include the one who put all things in subjection under him. $_{28}$ When all things are subjected to him, then the Son himself will

[25] For further discussion of this uncertainty as to the timing of resurrection in first-century Judaism, see the article "Resurrection," in *Encyclopedia Judaica* (cited in nt. 19 above).

[26] See Ps. 8:6.

also be subjected to the one who put all things in subjection under him, so that God may be all in all.

Paul in 1 Cor. 15:23 tells the Corinthians what he also told the Thessalonians—that those who belong to Christ will be raised at the *inauguration* of his coming kingdom, which he will establish "at his coming," when he takes up his glorious reign on the earth (cf. Mt. 16:27; 19:28; 25:31; Mk 8:38; Lk. 9:26; Col. 3:4; 1 Thess. 1:9; 2 Thess. 2:12). Paul has the opportunity here—as in 1 Thessalonians—to characterize Christ's coming as the occasion of a universal resurrection and judgment of all humanity, but this is not how he chooses to present the situation. His assurance to them is that the Parousia of Jesus signals the moment of resurrection for "those who belong to Christ."

Paul appears to be saying here that the "end," his shorthand for the final τάγμα, the last division of humanity for the purposes of resurrection, presents the opportunity for Christ to definitively defeat all residual enemies including death itself. Christ's defeat of death thus seems in some way to signal the *completion* of his work as Messiah. His reign, which must come into its full and glorious manifestation at his Parousia, may thus in Paul's mind have a mysterious "until" aspect. I'm not sure anyone thoroughly understands what he is saying in 1 Cor. 15.28, but a trinitarian, incarnational reading of this passage would tend to affirm that the Son, the eternal Word of God, will naturally continue to reign with his Father "world without end" (see below). Nevertheless there is a sense of completion when Christ finishes not just defeating, but *destroying*, all enemies including death itself (15.26). A closely analogous sense of completion attends the moment when John, after first seeing the total subjugation of the devil and all the unrepentant in Rev. 19:14–20:5, sees a final battle in which the resurgent devil and the resurrected unrepentant are together definitively both *defeated* and *annihilated* (Rev. 20:7-10). When he sees this denouement again under another figure a few verses later, John speaks of Death and Hades being "thrown into the lake of fire" (20:14). The final defeat and removal of death and all its forces that Paul describes somewhat elliptically and abstractly in 1 Cor. 15:26, John describes explicitly and concretely in Rev. 20:7-15.

Some readers may at this point be wanting to ask two related questions: 1. Don't New Testament authors teach that Jesus is reigning *now* in heaven? 2. Don't New Testament authors say that the reign of Jesus lasts forever, not simply for one age? Let's look at these issues in turn.

Christ's Kingdom—Here Now, or Not?

In answer to the first question, let me offer a broad New Testament answer first, then a more specifically exegetical one. Broadly speaking:

1. Jesus, as the divine Logos and Son of God, was reigning along with his Father and the Holy Spirit over the whole creation from its foundation.[27]
2. In an important sense, Jesus divested himself of his rulership over the creation as a whole when he took on human form and lived as a human being among us (Phil. 2:7-8; Jn 1:14; Rom. 8:3; 2 Cor. 8:9; Heb. 2:9-18; 4:7-8).[28] At the same time, he remained *entitled* to the full authority that is inherent in his Sonship.[29]
3. After his ascension Jesus took up again the divine rulership over the entire creation that is his by right, and he will continue to possess that right forever without end. In that sense, Jesus, together with the Father, is now again ruling over the entire creation.[30]

[27] Jn 1:1; 1 Cor. 8:6; Col. 1:15-18a; Heb. 1:2; 3:3-4.
[28] Admitting this seems essential in order to avoid *Docetism*, the doctrine that affirms that Jesus was not really human, but only appeared to be so. Orthodox Christology insists that Jesus was not masquerading as a human being—he *was* a human being, who humbly assumed our form and lived within the limitations and potentialities that our created design implies. We are not designed to be capable of understanding and overseeing every intimate aspect of the entire creation.
[29] Mt. 11:27; Lk. 10:22; Jn 3:35; 13:3; 17:2.
[30] Mt. 28:18-20; [Mk 16:9]; Rom. 8:34; 9:5; Eph. 1:20-22; 4:10; Phil. 2:9-11; Col. 3:1; Heb. 1:3-10; 10:12-13; 12:2; Rev. 3:21; 7:17.

According to many and varied New Testament sources, Jesus now reigns in heaven with his Father. Does this, by itself, indicate that Christians should understand the current age—the age between his ascension and his coming again in glory—as the messianic age prophesied by the OT prophets and by Jesus himself? It certainly does not. In order to be clear about this issue we must first recognize the distinction between Jesus' natural rights and identity as the Son of God on the one hand, and the outworking of his messianic ministry in human history and destiny on the other hand. In other words, expressions in the New Testament such as those in (3) above, which characterize the royal rights and privileges that Jesus now enjoys as the divine Son, do not by themselves tell us anything about the relationship between this age and the age(s) to come in terms of Christ's rulership as Messiah. Jesus now sits with his Father on the throne of the universe because he is God the Son. He has won the victory over sin, and he has proven himself worthy to be Messiah, God's chosen king and savior for humanity. But Jesus was *already* Messiah throughout his incarnate ministry of preaching, service and suffering, and he now *continues* his ministry of preaching, service and suffering on the earth through his body, the community of those who follow him.

Thus we may say that when Jesus comes in glory, at the transition-point between this age and the age to come, he will reign as Messiah on the renewed earth with his resurrected saints. Jesus and the New Testament writers insist again and again that these two modes of the divine messianic plan must happen in order: first comes the phase of preaching, humble service, and suffering—for Jesus, then for the community of his followers for the remainder of this age—*then* comes their glorious, resurrected reign in a renewed creation. The end of this age, the changing of the ages, and the inauguration of the messianic age lie in the future in relation to our own time as his mortal followers. Two passages will suffice to illustrate this point:

Mt. 28:18-20

> 18 ...All authority in heaven and on earth has been given to me. 19 Go therefore and make disciples of all nations, baptizing them in the name of the Father and of the Son and of the Holy Spirit, 20 and teaching them to obey

> everything that I have commanded you. And remember, I am with you always, to the end of the age.

2 Tim. 2:8-12a[31]

> 8 Remember Jesus Christ, raised from the dead, a descendant of David—that is my gospel, 9 for which I suffer hardship, even to the point of being chained like a criminal. But the word of God is not chained. 10 Therefore I endure everything for the sake of the elect, so that they may also obtain the salvation that is in Christ Jesus, with eternal glory. 11 The saying is sure:
>
> If we have died with him, we will also live with him;
> 12 if we endure, we will also reign with him.

The Christian community's ministry of preaching and service in the world—in humble vulnerability, often in the midst of persecution, after the pattern of Jesus' own ministry—constitutes the current phase of God's and Jesus' plan for the salvation of humanity and for the demonstration of God's justice and love on the earth.[32] It is a foundational mistake to overwrite, on the basis of scriptures such as those in (3) above, clearly futuristic messianic age prophecies in the OT and teachings in the NT that tie in closely with such OT prophecies. It is true that Jesus now rules—just as he did before his incarnation—and that he oversees, as the resurrected and ascended Messiah, his followers' continuation of his ministry of preaching and service in a sinful and violent world. However, his current divine and messianic authority does not at all imply that we should regard his rulership in the present age as the principal fulfillment of messianic age prophecies in both testaments. To make that conclusion, we would need explicit NT teaching to the effect that the current age of mortality and pervasive sin that we refer to as human history somehow paradoxically fulfills prophecies such as Ps. 2:8-12; 45:1-7; 110:1-6; Isa. 9:6-7; 11:6-12; 24:21–27:5; Jer. 23:5-6; Dan. 7:8-14, 17-18, 22-27; Mic. 5:2-5a. To the contrary, Jesus and the New Testament authors look upon

[31] See, similarly, Rom. 5:3-5; 6:5, 8; 8:17, 35-36; Phil. 1:29; Heb. 12:1-11; 1 Pet. 1:5-7; 4:13.

[32] See e.g. Acts 1:6-8, which serves as a kind of program for the book's entire account of the ministry of the apostles and the newborn community of Jesus.

this age as an evil—and frankly dangerous—age, in which malevolent human and angelic forces have a strong presence and influence,[33] and they *look ahead*, to the Parousia of Jesus, for the defeat of evil, the renewal of the world, and the fulfillment of the messianic age promises of peace, righteousness, and universal harmony. The following selection of passages illustrates this perspective.

Acts 3:19-21

> 19 Repent therefore, and turn to God so that your sins may be wiped out, 20 so that times of refreshing may come from the presence of the Lord, and that he may send the Messiah appointed for you, that is, Jesus, 21 who must remain in heaven until the time of universal restoration that God announced long ago through his holy prophets.

Heb. 10:35-39

> 35 Do not, therefore, abandon that confidence of yours; it brings a great reward. 36 For you need endurance, so that when you have done the will of God, you may receive what was promised. 37 For yet
>
> "in a very little while,
> the one who is coming will come and will not delay;
> 38 but my righteous one will live by faith.
> My soul takes no pleasure in anyone who shrinks back."[34]
>
> 39 But we are not among those who shrink back and so are lost, but among those who have faith and so are saved.[35]

Rom. 8:18-21

> 18 I consider that the sufferings of this present time are not worth comparing with the glory about to be revealed to us. 19 For the creation waits with eager longing for[36] the

[33] See 2 Cor. 4:4; Gal. 1:4; Eph. 2:2; 6:12; 1 Jn 2:15-17; 5:19-20.

[34] Traditionally: "And my righteous one will live on the basis of [his] faith; and if he shrinks back, my soul is not pleased with him" (Hab. 2:3-4 LXX).

[35] Lit. "faith, to the preservation of life/soul."

[36] Lit. "For the earnest expectation of the creation is looking forward to."

> revealing of the children of God; 20 for the creation was subjected to futility,[37] not of its own will but by the will of the one who subjected it, in hope 21 that the creation itself will be set free from its bondage to decay and will obtain the freedom of the glory of the children of God.

To summarize, a broad study of the New Testament reveals agreement that (1) Jesus does indeed now reign in heaven, and that (2) the current age, which follows his resurrection and ascension, *is not* the prophesied messianic age. Jesus is Messiah, humankind's and creation's King and Savior, but his and his Father's kingdom has not yet come.[38] As Jesus himself prophesies,

Mt. 19:28-30

> 28 Truly I tell you, at the renewal of all things, when the Son of Man is seated on the throne of his glory, you who have followed me will also sit on twelve thrones, judging the twelve tribes of Israel. 29 And everyone who has left houses or brothers or sisters or father or mother or children or fields, for my name's sake, will receive a hundredfold, and will inherit eternal life. 30 But many who are first will be last, and the last will be first.

This is how Jesus characterizes the messianic age. The "first," who will be "last" in that age, are those who enjoy relative status and affluence in this present age, or, in other words, those who are the winners in the current unjust economic and social order. On the other hand, those who give up their homes, their wealth, and their familial safety net—which is to say, those willing, on Jesus' instructions, to put at risk everything that gives them privilege, status, and security in this present age—will be rewarded in the age to come with vastly more than they

[37] Or "human folly," "vanity," "emptiness," or "foolishness."

[38] This principle is illustrated by the very words that Jesus teaches his followers to pray: "Let your kingdom come! Let your will be done—on earth just as it is in heaven!" (Mt. 5:10 || Lk. 11:2). See also, for example, Lk. 19:11-12, a parable that characterizes the remainder of this age as the period *between* (1) God's announcement of his selection of Jesus as Messiah, and (2) the moment when Jesus returns with power to defeat his enemies and to reign.

gave up, and they will receive resurrection life. This, our contemporary age, is the age of risk-taking, faith, and obedience; "that age" is the age of reigning in resurrection life with Christ. Mistaking the former for the latter is a mistake only the "first" can make.[39]

As I mentioned above, Jesus and a number of New Testament authors go well beyond a mere denial that this age is to be understood as the prophesied messianic kingdom, declaring that "the world" is essentially hostile to God, that this is an evil age, and that the current world and age are run by evil forces. For example:

Jn 15:18-19

> 18 If the world hates you, be aware that it hated me before it hated you. 19 If you belonged to the world, the world would love you as its own. Because you do not belong to the world, but I have chosen you out of the world—therefore the world hates you.

2 Cor. 4:3-4

> 3 And even if our gospel is veiled, it is veiled to those who are perishing. 4 In their case the god of this world has blinded the minds of the unbelievers, to keep them from seeing the light of the gospel of the glory of Christ, who is the image of God.

Gal. 1:3-4

> 3 Grace to you and peace from God our Father and the Lord Jesus Christ, 4 who gave himself for our sins to set us free from the present evil age, according to the will of our God and Father.

[39] For more on the subject of whether, to what extent, and in what ways the ministry of Jesus and his followers in this age fulfill OT hopes of a golden age of God's kingdom (also known as the issue of "realized eschatology"), see Mealy, *End of the Unrepentant* (see p. 29 nt. 44 above), Chapter 5, "The Changing of the Ages in the New Testament," 139-49. It is to be noted that postmillennial schemes including partial preterism are equally vulnerable to this analysis.

Eph. 2:1-2; 6:11-12

1 You were dead through the trespasses and sins 2 in which you once lived, following the course of this world, following the ruler of the power of the air, the spirit that is now at work among those who are disobedient.[40]

11 Put on the whole armor of God, so that you may be able to stand against the wiles of the devil. 12 For our struggle is not against enemies of blood and flesh, but against the rulers, against the authorities, against the cosmic powers of this present darkness, against the spiritual forces of evil in the heavenly places.

Jas 4:4

4 Adulterers! Do you not know that friendship with the world is enmity with God? Therefore whoever wishes to be a friend of the world becomes an enemy of God.

1 Jn 2:15-17, 3:13; 5:19

15 Do not love the world or the things in the world. The love of the Father is not in those who love the world; 16 for all that is in the world—the desire of the flesh, the desire of the eyes, the pride in riches—comes not from the Father but from the world. 17 And the world and its desire[41] are passing away, but those who do the will of God live forever.

13 Do not be astonished, brothers and sisters, that the world hates you.

19 We know that we are God's children,[42] and that the whole world lies under the power of the evil one.

[40] Lit. "in the children of disobedience." This is a Hebrew expression—compare "children of this world" and "children of light" (Luke 16:8).
[41] Or "lusts," or "cravings."
[42] Lit. "we are from God."

Christ's Coming Kingdom: Does it Last for One Age, or Does it Last Forever?

This second question turns out to hinge on a false dilemma, a dilemma that only arises when one espouses a conception of time that is foreign to the Hebrew and Christian scriptures. Here is the problem: interpreters commonly speak as though there were such a thing an "eternal state" that lasts "forever," but the biblical writers never express the idea of one endless and undifferentiated age of "eternity." Instead, they speak about time—past, present, and future—in terms of an indefinitely extended sequence of eras or ages. Thus, to speak biblically, we would have to affirm Christ's messianic kingdom does indeed last for the age to come, which is bounded in time. But we would also go on to affirm that Christ's kingdom continues *beyond* the age to come, into and throughout "the ages of the ages."

Let me give a specific and clear example. In the vision of Daniel 7, "one like a son of man"[43] is presented before the royal court of God and receives authority to reign (Dan. 7:13–14). In that scene, the divine court has been convened to determine what people(s) and what nation(s) should receive the authority to rule the earth in the age to come. A double verdict is passed: (1) the "fourth beast," the final world-dominating empire of human history, has its empire taken away, and it is destroyed by fire, and (2) the kingdom is handed over to "the people of the saints of the Most High" (Dan. 7:26–28). Their kingdom (which Christians also understand to be Jesus Christ's messianic kingdom) lasts for the age then being inaugurated, and also goes on to extend through an indefinite succession of following ages:

Dan. 7:18 (following the Aramaic and Old Greek)

> [18] And the saints of the Most High will receive the kingdom, and they will possess the kingdom for the age, and for the age of the ages.[44]

[43] More idiomatically, "what looked like a human being," or simply "a human figure." Christians, including many NT writers, typically understand this figure to represent Jesus Christ.

[44] Dan. 7:18, my translation. Here is the Greek, which follows the Aramaic closely: Καὶ παραλήψονται τὴν βασιλείαν ἅγιοι ὑψίστου καὶ καθέξουσι τὴν βασιλείαν ἕως τοῦ αἰῶνος καὶ ἕως τοῦ αἰῶνος τῶν αἰώνων.

Daniel here prophesies the coming of an age of renewal that will be brought in by the sovereign act of God as judge. After putting a stop to human history, God will commission the saints to rule the world for the age that then dawns, *and for all subsequent ages*. The distinction between the age to come and the ages that follow that age is completely obscured by the way in which almost all English translations customarily render this and similar passages. Here, for example, is the NRSV translation of the above verse from the original Aramaic:

> 18 But the holy ones of the Most High shall receive the kingdom and possess the kingdom forever—forever and ever.

And here is the NETS translation of the above verse in the Old Greek:

> 18 And the saints of the Most High will receive the kingdom and possess the kingdom forever—forever and ever.[45]

This pattern holds consistently throughout our English Bibles. Typically, expressions that would literally be translated "for the age" are translated "forever," and expressions that would literally be translated "for the age(s) of the ages" are translated "forever and ever" or "forevermore." Observe, however, what a difference it makes when this non-biblical phraseology is replaced with native biblical language:

Rom. 16:27 (my translation)

> 27 To the One Wise God, through Jesus Christ, be the glory to the ages![46] Amen.

Paul's blessing here shows that he shares with the author of Daniel (see Dan. 7:18; 12:3, Old Greek) the conception that the

[45] Dan. 7:14, Old Greek, according to *A New English Translation of the Septuagint*, ©2007 by the International Organization for Septuagint and Cognate Studies, Inc., used by permission of Oxford University Press. All rights reserved.

[46] Some early mss have, "to the ages of the ages." NRSV has "to the only wise God, through Jesus Christ, to whom be the glory forever!"

world to come contains an indefinite sequence of future ages, not just one.

1 Cor. 2:7

> 7 But we speak God's wisdom, secret and hidden, which God decreed before the ages for our glory.

Paul thinks of the past—as well as the future—as being marked by division into various ages. See similarly 1 Cor. 10:11, where he refers to believers as those "upon whom the ends of the ages have come."

Eph. 1:21

> 21 ...far above all rule and authority and power and dominion, and above every name that is named, not only in this age but also in the age to come.

Eph. 2:7

> 7 ...so that in the ages to come he might show the immeasurable riches of his grace in kindness toward us in Christ Jesus.

You can see from this pair of verses in Ephesians that Paul is comfortable talking about *the age* and *the ages* to come. If he affirms that Christ will rule in the age to come, that is not at all an affirmation that the age to come lasts forever, nor is it a denial that Christ will continue to rule throughout the endless ages that follow the age to come.

Heb. 1:1-2

> 1 Long ago God spoke to our ancestors in many and various ways by the prophets, 2 but in these last days he has spoken to us by a Son, whom he appointed heir of all things, through whom he also created the worlds.[47]

Heb. 9:26 (my translation)

> 26 But now he [Christ] has appeared once, at the wrapping up of the ages.[48]

[47] Lit. "the ages."

[48] NRSV undertranslates, "But as it is, he has appeared once for all at the end of the age..." (treating the plural of αἰών, "age," as though it were singular).

Like Paul, the author of Hebrews views looks upon the world's history as a sequence of ages. He also looks ahead to an indefinite series of future ages:

Heb. 13:8 (my translation)

> 8 Jesus Christ is the same yesterday, today, and for all the ages.[49]

Peter speaks just the same way:

1 Pet. 1:20

> 20 He was destined before the foundation of the world, but was revealed at the end of the ages for your sake.

1 Pet. 4:11 (my translation)

> 11 To him [Jesus] belong glory and dominion, to the ages of the ages.[50]

Jude refers in the following single statement to former ages, the present age, and all the ages to come:

Jude 25 (my translation)

> 25 To the One God our savior, through Jesus Christ our Lord, be glory, greatness, power, and authority—before every age, and now, and to all the ages.[51] Amen.

And of course John:

Rev. 22:4-5 (my translation)

> 4 ...and they [the saints] are going to see his face 5 ...and they're going to reign for the ages of the ages.[52]

There are more than a dozen similar examples in the New Testament. To summarize the force of this information, there is nothing out of sync with the rest of the New Testament in the idea that the thousand years of Revelation 20 follows the future

[49] NRSV has "Jesus Christ is the same yesterday and today and forever." Gr. Ἰησοῦς Χριστὸς ἐχθὲς καὶ σήμερον ὁ αὐτός καὶ εἰς τοὺς αἰῶνας.
[50] NRSV has "To him belong glory and the power forever and ever."
[51] NRSV has "before all time and now and forever." Gr. πρὸ παντὸς τοῦ αἰῶνος καὶ νῦν καὶ εἰς πάντας τοὺς αἰῶνας.
[52] NRSV has "and they will reign forever and ever."

Parousia of God and Christ. There simply is *no* biblical principle according to which the age following the Parousia is itself everlasting, extending into eternity without any segmentation into further ages.

Chapters 1–4: Summary of Results

In Chapter 1 we've presented a straightforward positive exposition of Rev. 19:5–21:8. This exposition demonstrates, by taking fully into account the many interpretive road signs that John himself supplies, that new creation millennialism provides a natural and theologically meaningful reading of this whole extended passage. One of the difficulties that interpreters have long expressed in relation to premillennialism is that there doesn't seem to be a *purpose* for such a period as a future millennium. Our exposition has revealed a theologically coherent and meaningful rationale for the millennium within God's overall plan of salvation and judgment.

We've shown in Chapter 2 that the historic premillennial reading of Revelation 20 fails. Its key assumptions—that ordinary mortal human beings survive the Parousia of Jesus, and that the coming of the New Jerusalem and the new creation occur only after the millennium—not only blatantly conflict with teachings elsewhere in the New Testament, but they are ruled out by clear evidences within the Book of Revelation itself.[53]

We've shown in Chapter 3 that the amillennial reading of Revelation 20 fails. It suffers from three major weaknesses—one of them serious, and the other two independently fatal. It unavoidably leads to gross contradictions within Revelation, and it requires making an identification between two scenes (Rev. 12:1-17; 20:1-3) that no unbiased reader could ever make.

In Chapter 4 we've disproven the oft-repeated assertion that the New Testament outside of Revelation 20:4-6 contains no evidence of the idea of a selective resurrection at the Parousia of Jesus for the faithful alone. To the person who does not bring to Jesus' remarks in Lk. 20:35 a prior hostility to the very possibility of such an idea, it is evident Jesus himself affirms that

[53] These weaknesses attend dispensational premillennialism to the same degree as they attend historic premillennialism.

only those judged "worthy" will be raised from among the dead to take part in the age to come. And if Jesus does indeed affirm this, then Paul's way of talking about his own resurrection hope (Phil. 3:10-11), the resurrection hope of the Thessalonians (1 Thess. 4:13-17), and his understanding of God's plan to resurrect all through Christ in (1 Cor. 15:22-25) all make excellent sense according to this split-resurrection paradigm.[54]

We've gone on to show that, even if we exclude the Book of Revelation, with its particularly negative view of the current age, we find that Jesus and the New Testament writers *do not* look upon this age or any part of it as the glorious messianic age prophesied in the OT. They instead see it as an age in which first Jesus, then his faithful followers, bear powerful witness to the truth of God in a hostile, evil, and even demonically and satanically infested world. This is not the age of worldly success, riches, and supremacy for Christ and his faithful ones, but the age of humble witness-bearing, service, and endurance under persecution.[55]

Lastly we've shown that the supposed contradiction between an everlasting age to come and a temporally-bounded age to come (as in Rev. 20:1-10) dissolves upon an unbiased examination of the biblical terminology of "ages." In Revelation itself, as in Dan. 7:18, when the Son of Man comes, it is affirmed both that the saints reign for the coming age (cf. Rev. 20:4, 6) and that they reign "for the ages of the ages" (Rev. 22:5).[56] These two affirmations simply do not stand in tension with one another.

[54] Admittedly, Jesus' statement in Jn 5:28-29 sits more comfortably with the idea of a single general resurrection: "...the hour is coming when all who are in their graves will hear his voice and will come out—those who have done good, to the resurrection of life, and those who have done evil, to the resurrection of condemnation." On the other hand, Jesus has in the previous breath said that the "hour" (i.e. the moment) of resurrection amounts to an *era* of resurrection that starts with his own ministry (Jn 5:25): "...the hour is coming, *and is now here*, when the dead will hear the voice of the Son of God, and those who hear will live." In my view, Jn 5:28-29 contains more room for ambiguity than either Lk. 20:35-36 or Rev. 20. For more on this issue see Mealy, *End of the Unrepentant* (see p. 29 nt. 44 above), 164-67,

[55] On this, see, most pointedly, Lk. 6:20-26; Jas. 4:13–5:11; Rev. 3:14-22.

[56] Gr. εἰς τοὺς αἰῶνας τῶν αἰώνων.

Conclusion

The Results of This Study

As promised, I have demonstrated the viability of the new creation millennialism interpretive paradigm by providing a continuous and straightforward exposition of Rev. 19:5–21:8, which is to say, the millennium passage itself (Rev. 20:1-10), together with a generous portion of context on either side. This interpretive paradigm avoids the insuperable difficulties of amillennialism, historic premillennialism, and what might be called the lifeless-earth millennialism espoused by Seventh Day Adventist interpreters.

It does not impose, in contradiction to the strong indications in Rev. 21:1-8 and elsewhere in Revelation, a thousand-year delay between the Parousia of God and Jesus and (1) the renewal of the cosmos, (2) the wedding of the Lamb and the Bride, (3) the coming to earth of the New Jerusalem, (4) the coming to earth and reigning upon the earth of God, Jesus, and the faithful, and (5) final and total unification between God and redeemed humanity.

It does not propose, in contradiction to the explicit teaching of Jesus (Lk. 20:35) and the strong indications in Rev. 6:12-17, Rev. 19:17-21, and elsewhere in Revelation, that many unrepentant human beings will survive the Parousia to enter the millennial period as mortals.

It does not require, in defiance of the obvious and natural flow of the narrative, that the capture and imprisonment of Satan (Rev. 20:1-3) be split off from the capture and destruction of his agents, the beast and the false prophet, and the capture and imprisonment of the kings of the earth (Rev. 19:17-21; cf. Isa. 24:21-23).

It does not attempt, in defiance of all rational principles of narrative interpretation, to equate the capture, chaining, and imprisonment of Satan in the underworld abyss (Rev. 20:1-3) with the expulsion of Satan from heaven to earth in Rev. 12:1–13:1.

It does not relegate the thousand-year imprisonment of Satan to the period before the Parousia, which results in out-and-out contradiction no matter how you place it. If you place it before the appearance of the beast, then the thousand-year reign of the saints executed by the beast (20:4) takes place before the beast ever appears. But if you plot it *during* or *after* the career of the beast, then the period characterized by Satan's greatest success ever in deceiving humanity so as to get them to make war on the saints (through the beast) gets plotted on top of the period in which Satan is sitting chained up and sealed in the prison of the abyss, unable to deceive the nations any longer.

Positively speaking, this exposition accomplishes many things:

It reads the text attentively—in a way that is thoroughly and consistently responsive to the dense network of interpretive clues that John laces into his narrative.

It detects and follows up cross-references—verbal hints that John regularly provides to help readers relate new visions to visions that he has previously narrated. It also detects and responds appropriately to the cross-references that John constantly provides to the end-times visions of earlier prophets, especially Isaiah 24–27, Daniel 7, and Ezekiel 37–39.

It makes better sense—more substantial and more broadly grounded theological sense—of the millennium than amillennialism, historic premillennialism, or lifeless-earth millennialism.

It achieves a coherent reading that does not suffer from any major contradictions, either with other texts in Revelation or texts dealing with the same themes elsewhere in the New Testament.[1] Admittedly, new creation millennialism, by interpreting the new creation and the coming to earth of the New Jerusalem as a vision of the Parousia, results in chronological tension or cosmological paradox in Revelation. For when the new creation is understood to *begin* the thousand-year reign, John's statement that "there is no sea anymore" (Rev. 21:1) seems to conflict with his previous statement that, at the post-thousand-year resurrection of the unrepentant, "the sea gave up the dead that were in it" (Rev. 20:13). This, however, becomes a non-issue if the "sea" that was no longer there, as John looked up and saw the New Jerusalem descending in the new creation, was the glassy sea of separation between heaven and earth (see the exposition of Rev. 21:1-3). Even if John is referring to the earthly sea in 21:1, the tension between 21:1 and 20:13 is significantly lessened when we note that the central water-related image of the new creation is River of the Water of Life (22:1-2), which presumably flows out to fill the virgin seabed of the new creation. The sea of the new creation thus has the potential to symbolize the life-giving power of God (cf. Ezek. 47:8-9; Rev. 22:1-2) and a place out of which dead people rise and live, rather than a place into which living people fall and die.

Concluding Theological Remarks

One of the great embarrassments of the Christian faith lies in the stark contradiction between its message of a God of infinite love and grace and its doctrine that God has a plan to torment forever those who do not love him in return. This doctrine has hung like an albatross around the neck of Christian profession for two millennia. New creation millennialism, by reading the final chapters of Revelation with proper sensitivity to their own narrative logic and to their literary relationship with sister prophetic passages in Isaiah (24–27, 34, 65–66), ends up demolishing the textual foundation for the harmful doctrine of an infinitely vindictive God. In its place it reveals the image of a God of astonishing grace, a God who values the life of the

[1] For a discussion of passages such as Mt. 25:31-46 (esp. cf. 25:41; Isa. 24:21-22); Mt. 5:26 || Lk. 12:59; Mt. 12:41-42 || Lk. 11:31-32; Mk 9:42-48 || Mt. 5:29-30, see chs. 2–7 in *The End of the Unrepentant* (see p. 29 nt. 44, above).

unrepentant to the point of granting them a fresh start and an open invitation to take part in the life of the new creation. People always seem to raise two questions when presented with this reading: (1) How could it be that human beings, granted a truly new start and free access to the wondrous world of the new creation, would not come to reconciling faith and love for God? (2) Why, if this nigh-on-unbelievable persistence of human unrepentance and enmity were foreknown by God, would God resurrect the "rest of the dead" and give them the offer of everlasting life?

The first question is not actually a new question; it goes all the way back to the story of Adam and Eve in the Garden of Eden. How, when the first human beings had been granted free access to the gift of everlasting life in the "new creation" (Gen. 2), could they listen to the anti-gospel of the "old serpent" (Gen. 3:1-5; Rev. 20:2, 7-8)? How could they choose to believe—against all evidence—that God, rather than warning them of the deadliness of the forbidden fruit in order to protect them from harm, was instead stingily holding back some mysterious thing that pertained to their highest good? I submit that there has never been a rational answer to the mystery of the human choice to turn away from the love of the all-giving Creator and embrace cynicism, hatred, enmity, and selfishness. As it was in the beginning, John prophesies, so shall it be at the end. I admit that the scene revealed in Rev. 20:7-10 || Isa. 27:1-5 is a deeply unattractive ending to the story of the unrepentant from the human point of view, but it is by no means an unfamiliar ending. We human beings are famous among ourselves for preferring to deny, to project, and to self-justify to the very end—indeed, to go down in flames rather than accept grace and humbly begin again.

The second question goes to the heart of the mystery of grace. Yet a biblical answer is not far to seek: God gives human beings a taste life—and even resurrected life—regardless of whether they will ultimately spit it out, *because God loves them* (Ps. 145:8-9; Isa. 57:15-21). I recently watched a science fiction film in which one of the characters knows with absolute certainty that she will bear a child, and that that child will face a difficult illness and die before reaching adulthood. Nevertheless she fully embraces the whole process of engendering and nurturing that life without hesitation and without regret. Her certain knowledge of the future changes nothing, and her undiluted love remains unquestionable.

There is a greater, and far more troubling, question that rears its head when God's traditionally-imagined cruelty is taken away, and it is this: *Why does God give human beings such terrifying power to destroy and make miserable their own lives, the lives of one another, and the lives of other living things in the eco-system into which they were created?* To this question the New Testament gives answers that perhaps only faith will find even partially satisfying. In the first place, the gift of resurrection itself can repay beyond all imagination a stolen life, a broken, or a persecuted life (Rom. 8:18; 2 Cor. 4:17-18; Rev. 7:13-17; 22:1-5). But far deeper than this, the New Testament preaches that the Creator personally chose to take responsibility for the freedom granted the created ones by becoming one of them, and, in solidarity with them, facing the worst they could do to one another (Heb. 2:9-15; 5:1-10; Rev. 3:21; 5:1-10). Only that One has the standing to judge the living and the dead for the way they have treated one another and their world, and to repay each, with justice and grace, for everything they have suffered and caused others to suffer.

Appendix 1
Narrative Sections and Temporal Analysis That Underlie Chart 1

Rev. 4:1-2 “I heard a voice…” John’s time.

Rev. 4:3–5:14 The authorization of the Lamb. At Christ’s ascension and exaltation.

Rev. 6:1-11 The first five seals. Time of distress.

Rev. 6:12-17 The sixth seal. “Hide us from him who sits on the throne…” Parousia.

Rev. 7:1-8 The sealing of the 144,000. Time of distress.

Rev. 7:9-17 The numberless multitude before the throne. Parousia.

Rev. 8:1–9:21 First six trumpets. Final crisis.

Rev. 10:1-7 Vision of the great angel announcing the end. Parousia.

Rev. 10:8-11 “You must prophesy again…” John’s time.

Rev. 11:1-14 The two witnesses. Time of distress.

Rev. 11:15-19 The seventh trumpet. Parousia.

Rev. 12:1–13:18 The expulsion of the devil and the career of the beast. Time of distress.

Rev. 14:1-5 The triumphant stand of the 144,000 with Christ on Zion. Parousia.

Rev. 14:6-8 Final warnings to those who dwell on the earth. Final crisis.

Rev. 14:9-12 Warning that the followers of the beast will be tormented at the Parousia. Parousia.

Rev. 14:13 Blessing on those who die from now on. John's time.

Rev. 14:14-20 Two visions of the harvest of the earth. Parousia.

Rev. 15:1 Announcement of the seven bowls. Final crisis.

Rev. 15:2-4 Celebration of salvation and victory over the beast in heaven. Parousia.

Rev. 15:5–16:17 Bowls. Final crisis.

Rev. 16:18-21 Seventh bowl. Parousia.

Rev. 17:1–18:24 Judgment of Babylon the Great. Final crisis.

Rev. 19:1-21 "Hallelujah! Our Lord God, the All Powerful, now reigns!" Wedding announcement. Rider on a white horse. Parousia.

Rev. 20:1-3 Capture and imprisonment of Satan. Parousia.

Rev. 20:4-6 Reign of the witnesses of God and Christ. The thousand years.

Rev. 20:7-10 Resurgence and destruction of Satan and the unrepentant. After the thousand years.

Rev. 20:11-12 Recap of the judgment scene of 20:4-6, focus on negative judgment. Parousia.

Rev. 20:13-15 Final judgment of the unrepentant—recap of 20:7-10. After the thousand years.

Rev. 21:1–22:5 New creation and New Jerusalem. Parousia—and into the ages of the ages (22:5).

Rev. 22:6-11 Promises and warnings to the faithful. John's time.

Rev. 22:12-17 Announcements and promises of the Parousia. Parousia.

Rev. 22:18-21 Final words to the readers. John's time.

Appendix 2
Detailed Synopsis of Revelation and Isaiah 24–27

Isaiah	Revelation
5 The earth lies polluted under its inhabitants; for they have transgressed laws, violated the statutes, broken the everlasting covenant. 6 Therefore a curse devours the earth, and its inhabitants suffer for their guilt; therefore the inhabitants of the earth dwindled, and few people are left. (24:5-6)	8:7 …a third of the earth was burned up, and a third of the trees were burned up, and all green grass was burned up. … 9:18 By these three plagues a third of humankind was killed, by the fire and smoke and sulfur… 20 The rest of humankind, who were not killed by these plagues, did not repent of the works of their hands or give up worshiping demons and idols of gold and silver and bronze and

	stone and wood, which cannot see or hear or walk. [21] And they did not repent of their murders or their sorceries or their fornication or their thefts. (8:7; 9:18-21) [8] The fourth angel poured his bowl on the sun, and it was allowed to scorch people with fire; [9] they were scorched by the fierce heat, but they cursed the name of God, who had authority over these plagues, and they did not repent and give him glory. (16:8-9)
The mirth of the timbrels is stilled, the noise of the jubilant has ceased, the mirth of the lyre is stilled. (24:8)	[22] …and the sound of harpists and minstrels and of flutists and trumpeters will be heard in you no more…(18:22)
[14] They lift up their voices, they sing for joy; they shout from the west over the majesty of the LORD. [15] Therefore in the east give glory to the LORD;	[1] After this I heard what seemed to be the loud voice of a great multitude in heaven, saying, "Hallelujah!

in the coastlands of the sea glorify the name of the LORD, the God of Israel. 16 From the ends of the earth we hear songs of praise, of glory to the Righteous One. (24:14-16a)	Salvation and glory and power to our God, 2 for his judgments are true and just [righteous]…" (19:1-2)
16 But I say, I pine away, I pine away. Woe is me! For the treacherous deal treacherously, the treacherous deal very treacherously. (24:16b)	16 And the ten horns that you saw, they and the beast will hate the whore; they will make her desolate and naked; they will devour her flesh and burn her up with fire. (17:16)[1]
18 Whoever flees at the sound of the terror shall fall into the pit; and whoever climbs out of the pit shall be caught in the snare. For the windows of heaven are opened, and the foundations of the earth tremble. 19 The earth is utterly broken, the earth is torn asunder, the earth is violently shaken. 20 The earth staggers like a drunkard, it sways like a hut;	14 And every mountain and island was removed from its place. (6:14) 18 And there came… a violent earthquake, such as had not occurred since people were upon the earth, so violent was that earthquake… 20 And every island fled away, and no mountains were to be found; 21 and huge hailstones, each weighing about a hundred pounds,

[1] The beast used to be the emperor of the empire Babylon. John pictures his betrayal as the greatest act of treachery in the history of the world.

its transgression lies heavy upon it, and it falls, and will not rise again. (24:18-20)	dropped from heaven on people (16:18, 20-21)
21 On that day the LORD will punish the host of heaven, in heaven, and the kings of the earth, on the earth. 22 They will be gathered together as prisoners in a pit; they will be shut up in a prison, and after many days they will be punished. (24:21-22)	19 Then I saw the beast and the kings of the earth with their armies… [The beast is captured and cast in the lake of fire with the false prophet.] 21 And the rest were killed by the sword of the rider on the horse, the sword that came from his mouth; and all the birds were gorged with their flesh. [Satan is captured and imprisoned in the underworld for a thousand years.] (19:19–20:3)
23 The moon will be dismayed, the sun ashamed; for the LORD Almighty will reign on Mount Zion and in Jerusalem, and before its elders—with great glory. (24:23)	23 And the city has no need of sun or moon to shine on it, for the glory of God is its light, and its lamp is the Lamb. 5 And there will be no more night; they need no light of lamp or sun, for the Lord God will be their light, and they will reign forever

	and ever. (21:23; 22:5) [Christ reigns with his faithful ones in "the Beloved City"] (20:4, 6, 9; 21:1-2, 9-27)
1 O LORD, you are my God; I will exalt you, I will praise your name… 2 For you have made the city a heap, the fortified city a ruin; the palace of aliens is a city no more, it will never be rebuilt. (25:1-2)	2 Fallen, fallen is Babylon the great! 21 …Babylon the great city will be thrown down, and will be found no more… 3 Hallelujah! The smoke goes up from her forever and ever![2] (18:2, 21; 19:3)
7 And he will destroy on this mountain [Mt. Zion, symbolic of Jerusalem] the shroud that is cast over all peoples, the sheet that is spread over all nations;	1 …and the sea was no more…[3] 3 And I heard a loud voice from the throne saying,

[2] The visual image of smoke going up from ruins forever without end is a way of expressing the assurance that these ruins will never be rebuilt (see e.g. Isa.34:8-10).

[3] In this particular context, it appears that John is referring to the sea of glass that functions as a ceiling to the human world and a floor to the heavenly throne room of God. That "sea" creates both a separation and a veil between humanity and God (see Exod. 24:10; Ezek. 1:22; 10:1; Rev. 4:1, 6; 6:14; 15:2; 19:11; 21:21). It is now removed, and God and all the faithful in heaven, i.e. the New Jerusalem, are seen to come down and make their habitation on the earth.

[8] he will swallow up death forever. Then the Lord GOD will wipe away the tears from all faces. (25:7-8)	See, the home [lit. *tent*] of God is among mortals. He will dwell with them; they will be his people[s], and God himself will be with them; [4] he will wipe every tear from their eyes. Death will be no more… (21:1-4)
[10] If favor is shown to the wicked, they do not learn righteousness; in the land of uprightness they deal perversely and do not see the majesty of the LORD. (26:10)	[8] [Satan deceives the newly resurrected unrepentant, gathering them for battle.] [9] They marched up over the breadth of the earth and surrounded the camp of the saints and the beloved city. (20:7-9)
[11] O LORD, your hand is lifted up, but they do not see it. Let them see your zeal for your people, and be ashamed. Let the fire for your adversaries consume them. (26:11)	[10] And fire came down from heaven and consumed them. (20:10)

[19] Your dead shall live, their corpses shall rise. [Heb: "my corpse, they shall rise!"] O dwellers in the dust, awake and sing for joy! For your dew is a radiant dew, and the earth will give birth to those long dead. (26:19)	[4] [Those killed by the beast for their testimony] came alive and ruled with Christ for a thousand years. (20:4)
[13] The dead [the oppressors of the faithful, 26:13] do not live; shades do not rise— because you have punished and destroyed them, and wiped out all memory of them. (26:14)	[5] The rest of the dead did not come to life until the thousand years were ended. (20:5)
[20] Come, my people, enter your chambers, and shut your doors behind you; hide yourselves for a little while until the wrath is past. [21] For the LORD comes out from his place to punish the inhabitants of the earth for their iniquity; the earth will disclose the blood shed on it, and will no longer cover its slain. (26:20-21)	[9] They marched up over the breadth of the earth and surrounded the camp of the saints and the beloved city. [10] And fire came down from heaven and consumed them. (20:9-10)

1 On that day the LORD with his cruel and great and strong sword will punish Leviathan the fleeing serpent, Leviathan the twisting serpent, and he will kill the dragon that is in the sea. (27:1)	2 [An angel] seized the dragon, that ancient serpent, who is the Devil and Satan, and bound him for a thousand years. 10 And the devil who had deceived them was thrown into the lake of fire and sulfur, where the beast and the false prophet were, and they will be tormented day and night forever and ever. (20:2, 10)
2 A pleasant vineyard,[4] sing of it! 3 I, the LORD, am its keeper; I water it at all times. Lest anyone bring harm on it, I keep watch over it night and day. 4 I have no wrath— Will someone give me thorns and briers to battle? I will stamp on them, I will burn them up together. 5 Instead, let them lay hold of my protection. Let them make peace with me; let them make peace with me. (27:2-5, my trans.)	9 They marched up over the breadth of the earth and surrounded the camp of the saints and the beloved city. 10 And fire came down from heaven and consumed them. (20:9-10)

[4] In Isaiah this symbolizes the people of God. See Isa. 5:1-7.

Appendix 3
A Brief Introduction to Previous Proponents of New Creation Millennialism

New creation millennialism may be unfamiliar to most contemporary readers, but it is not in fact new at all. Indeed, this (or something closely akin to it) appears to be the dominant view of the first post-New Testament generation of Christian writers known as "the apostolic fathers." This includes in particular those who lived in the region of the seven churches to which Revelation was addressed (Rev. 1:10; 21–3:21).

Early Church (70–300 CE)

Papias of Hierapolis (fl. c. 105–130 CE)

As far as is known, Papias is the earliest influential interpreter of Revelation. He lived a mere six miles from Laodicea (Rev. 1:11; 3:14), and Irenaeus describes him as "a hearer of John."[1] He believes in a future, earthly millennium, which earns him contempt from Eusebius:

[1] *Against Heresies* 5.33.4. Dionysius of Alexandria (d. 264 CE), wanting to discredit Papias because of the latter's belief that the millennium would begin when Jesus returned, tried to argue that the "John" whom Papias knew was not John the author of Revelation. See Eusebius, *Hist. Eccl.* (*Ecclesiastical History*) 7.25.6-17. His arguments are contrived.

> ...he [Papias] says that there will be a certain thousand years after the resurrection of the dead, when the kingdom of Christ will be set up bodily on this earth.[2]

Irenaeus attributes to Papias the following saying of Jesus, which speaks of the mind-boggling abundance of the earth in Christ's future kingdom:

> Each vine will have 10,000 branches, each branch 10,000 twigs, each twig 10,000 shoots, each shoot 10,000 clusters, each cluster 10,000 grapes, each grape will yield 25 measures of wine, and all the clusters will be crying, "I am a better cluster—please pick me and through me bless the Lord."[3]

Based on this statement, it is apparent that Papias envisioned the future millennial age both as being inaugurated by the miraculous renewal of the created world, and as being experienced by the faithful in the context of the (renewed) earth. His concept of the millennium was despised by the dominant theologians of later, ascetic-minded generations (such as Origen, Eusebius, and Augustine).[4] Thanks to their hostility, the five

[2] *Hist. Eccl.* 3.39:11-12, my translation. See also the translation and comments of J. Quasten, *Patrology* (2 vols.; Westminster, MD: The Newman Press, 1950), I, 4.

[3] Quoted by Irenaeus, *Against Heresies* 5.33:3. See also the *Syriac Apocalypse of Baruch* (*2 Baruch* 29:3-8), which attributes a similar saying to Baruch, secretary to Jeremiah. Papias collected a number of such *agrapha* (sg. *agraphon*), sayings reportedly spoken by Jesus but not written in the four gospels. That collection has perished, along with all his other writings, thanks to the severe anti-chiliastic (i.e. anti-premillennial) prejudice of later generations of church leaders.

[4] For Origen's eschatological views, see his *de Principiis* 2.2-3. For Eusebius, see the reference in nt. 2, above. For Augustine, note the following statement: "The evangelist John has spoken of these two resurrections in the book which is called the Apocalypse, but in such a way that some Christians do not understand the first of the two, and so construe the passage into ridiculous fancies. For the Apostle John says in the foresaid book, "And I saw an angel come down from heaven. . . . Blessed and holy is he that has part in the first resurrection: on such the second death has no power; but they shall be priests of God and of Christ, and shall reign with Him a thousand years" [Rev. xx. 1–6. The whole passage is quoted.] Those who, on the strength of this passage, have suspected that the first resurrection is future and bodily, have

books written by Papias (and the works of other premillennial theologians, such as Nepos of Arsinoe and Melito of Sardis) were completely suppressed and lost. We therefore lack any firm basis for knowing if Papias actually subscribed to a "crude and sensual" view of the millennium at all, or whether he understood Rev. 21:1-2 as having reference to the Parousia of God and Christ (as opposed to the period after the thousand years of Rev. 20:1-10). What we do know is that Papias expected the thousand-year reign of the saints to take place in the context of a miraculously renewed earth.

Epistle of Barnabas (c. 70–130 CE)

The author of the pseudonymous Epistle of Barnabas (written between 75 and 138) is traditionally understood to have been a believer in a future millennium, and develops his theology of history and the millennium on the basis of the six-day creation narrated in Genesis 1:1–2.4:

> ...the Lord will make an end of everything in six thousand years, for a day with him means a thousand years. ... So then, children, in six days (that is, in six thousand years) everything will be completed. "And he rested on

been moved, among other things, specially by the number of a thousand years, as if it were a fit thing that the saints should thus enjoy a kind of Sabbath-rest during that period, a holy leisure after the labors of the six thousand years since man was created, and was on account of his great sin dismissed from the blessedness of paradise into the woes of this mortal life, so that thus, as it is written, "One day is with the Lord as a thousand years, and a thousand years as one day," [2 Pet. 3:8] there should follow on the completion of six thousand years, as of six days, a kind of seventh-day Sabbath in the succeeding thousand years; and that it is for this purpose the saints rise, viz., to celebrate this Sabbath. And this opinion would not be objectionable, if it were believed that the joys of the saints in that Sabbath shall be spiritual, and consequent on the presence of God; for I myself, too, once held this opinion. But, as they assert that those who then rise again shall enjoy the leisure of immoderate carnal banquets, furnished with an amount of meat and drink such as not only to shock the feeling of the temperate, but even to surpass the measure of credulity itself, such assertions can be believed only by the carnal. They who do believe them are called by the spiritual Chiliasts, which we may literally reproduce by the name Millenarians" (*City of God* 20.7, from *Nicene and Post-Nicene Fathers* [First Series, 2, ed. Philip Schaff; trans. Marcus Dods; Buffalo, NY: Christian Literature Publishing Co., 1887).

> the seventh day." This means: when his Son comes he will destroy the time of the wicked one, and will judge the godless, and will change the sun and the moon and the stars, and then he will truly rest on the seventh day.[5]

Barnabas goes on to base the Christian's present self-preparation for the coming of Jesus upon the command to keep the Sabbath holy. Looking ahead to Jesus Christ's coming in glory, he says:

> ...we shall indeed keep it holy at that time, when we enjoy true rest, when we shall be able to do so because we have been made righteous ourselves and have received the promise, when there is no more sin, but all things have been made new by the Lord: then we shall be able to keep it holy because we ourselves have first been made holy. (15:7)

Next Barnabas explains Isa. 1:13, which condemns present celebrations of the Sabbath, by saying that the present reality is only a type of the final and eternal rest of the future:

> Do you see what he means? The present sabbaths are not acceptable to me, but that which I have made, in which I will give rest to all things and make the beginning of an eighth day, that is the beginning of another world. (15:8)

Here he clearly states the paradox that the seventh millennial day is at one and the same time the eighth day of the new creation: that is, he does not say of the millennium that it is the true eschatological Sabbath which is followed by the eternal eighth day of the new creation, but rather that it is the very day on which God renews all things. This is perhaps less obvious in English than in the Greek, which reads:

> οὐ τὰ σάββατα ἐμοὶ δεκτά, ἀλλὰ ὃ πεποίηκα, ἐν ᾧ καταπαύσας τὰ πάντα ἀρχὴν ἡμέρας ὀγδόης ποιήσω, ὅ ἐστιν ἄλλου κόσμου ἀρχήν.

[5] Ep. Barn. 15:4-5, trans. K. Lake, *Apostolic Fathers*, I. Further quotations will be from this source. See similarly Irenaeus, *Against Heresies* 5.18.33.

For Barnabas, the seventh millennial day (reckoned in terms of the present creation) is at the same time the inauguration of the eighth day of God's new creation. The millennium is God's final Sabbath rest from creating the world, in the sense that the course of human history itself has been part of his creative activity. Looking at it this way, God will not be able to rest finally until he has accomplished the salvation and perfection of the faithful and the renewal of the creation spoiled by the fall. Christ's coming in glory therefore signals the completion of God's redemptive work, and he can truly rest in the seventh millennium from the six-millennia-long work of reclaiming and perfecting his creation. The millennium is also the world's Sabbath, because for the first time it can rest, having been freed from sin and brought to perfection. At the same time, the millennium is an *eighth* day, or, in other words, it is *the first day in a new week of ages*, the beginning of a flawless new creation. For Barnabas, the seventh and eighth millennia *overlap* one another.

It is noteworthy that in the millennium, Barnabas sees the faithful ruling not over peoples and nations spared at Christ's coming in glory, but over the re-created and restored earth with its creatures, as God had intended in the beginning:

> And we have said above, "And let them increase and multiply and rule over the fishes." Who then is it who is now able to rule over beasts or fishes or the birds of heaven? For we ought to understand that to rule, implies authority, so that one may give commandments and have dominion. If then this does not happen at present he has told us when it will—when we ourselves also have been made perfect as heirs of the covenant of the Lord. (6:18-19; cf. also 6:13)

Melito, Bishop of Sardis (fl. c. 150–200 CE)

Melito was, according to patristics scholar Johannes Quasten, "one of the most venerable figures of the second century."[6] Jerome (*Comm. in Exod.* 36) affirms that Melito was a premillennialist, but Melito's direct statements on the question

[6] Quasten, *Patrology*, I, 242.

of the millennium have been lost, likely having been subjected to book-destruction thanks to the intense hostility of later theologians towards premillennialism. Obviously the fact that Melito resided in Sardis, one of the seven cities to which Revelation was addressed (Rev. 1:11; 3:1), makes him one of the persons closest, both in time and location, to the original book. Here is a quotation that appears to indicate that he was a new creation millennialist:

> There is a God, the Father of all, who never came into being, neither was ever made, and by whose will all things subsist. He also made the luminaries, that His works may see one another; and He conceals Himself in His power from all His works: for it is not permitted to any being subject to change to see Him who changes not. But such as are mindful of His words, and are admitted into that covenant which is unchangeable, 'they' see God—so far as it is possible for them to see Him. These also will have power to escape destruction, when the flood of fire comes upon all the world. For there was once a flood and a wind, and the great men were swept away by a violent blast from the north, but the just were left, for a demonstration of the truth. Again, at another time there was a flood of water, and all men and animals perished in the multitude of waters, but the just were preserved in an ark of wood by the command of God. So also will it be at the last time: there shall be a flood of fire, and the earth shall be burnt up, together with its mountains; and mankind shall be burnt up, along with the idols which they have made, and the carved images which they have worshipped; and the sea shall be burnt up, together with its islands; but the just shall be preserved from wrath, like as were their fellows of the ark from the waters of the deluge. And then shall those who have not known God, and those who have made them idols, bemoan themselves, when they shall see those

> idols of theirs being burnt up, together with themselves, and nothing shall be found to help them.[7]

Melito expects the fiery destruction of the entire present creation to happen at the end of this present age (as in 2 Pet. 3:3-13), thus there is clearly no room in his conception for ordinary people surviving to take part in the age to come. If, as would be natural, Melito understood the creation of the new heavens and the new earth to follow immediately upon their dissolution (as appears to be the assumption in 2 Pet. 3:13), then he would have been a new creation millennialist. Unfortunately, owing to the scarcity of existing fragments from Melito, there is no way of completely ruling out the possibility that he believed the world would remain in a state of destruction until after the millennium (as do the Seventh Day Adventists and the heirs to their interpretive tradition). Two things can be said, however: (1) no extant Christian work in the period up to and including Augustine's generation puts forward the idea that the earth will lie in a state of dissolution for a long time following the Parousia of Jesus, and (2) it is highly unlikely that Melito would have been silenced by having all his books destroyed if he had believed the millennial reign of the saints *had heaven as its setting*. After all, the specific thing about premillennialism that writers like Origen, Eusebius, Augustine, and Jerome found offensive was its *earthly* setting.

The Apocalypse of Elijah (c. 150–250 CE)

The Apocalypse of Elijah is another important witness to the way in which early Christians interpreted the millennium. It is Jewish-Christian and ascetic in character, and evinces close familiarity with Revelation. Just like (pseudo-) Barnabas, the author expects the destruction and re-creation of the heavens and earth to precede, rather than to follow, the millennium:

[7] Fragment from a discourse delivered in the presence of Antoninus Caesar, quoted from *Anti-Nicene Christian Library: Translations of the Writings of the Fathers Down to A.D. 325*. XXII. *The Works of Lactantius, Vol. II: Together with the Testaments of the Twelve Patriarchs and Fragments of the Second and Third Centuries* (trans. and ed. A. Roberts and J. Donaldson; Edinburgh: T. & T. Clark, 1871), 123-24.

> At that time the Christ will have compassion on those who are his. He will send his angels from heaven.... Those upon whose forehead is written the name of the Christ, upon whose right hand is the seal, both small and great, they will be taken on their wings and removed from the wrath. Then Gabriel and Uriel will be a column of light and go before them until they bring them to the holy land, and they will permit them to eat from the tree of life and to wear white garments, while the angels keep watch over them. They will neither hunger nor thirst, nor will the lawless one have power over them.
>
> He [the devil] will perish like a dragon which is without breath. He will be told, "Your time is up. Now you will perish with those who believed in you." They will be thrown into the deep pit, and it will be shut over them. At that time the Christ comes from heaven, the king together with all his saints. He burns the earth and spends a thousand years on it, because the sinners held sway over it. He will create a new heaven and a new earth. No devil or death exists in them. With the saints he will rule, descending and ascending. They will be with the angels always. They will be with the Christ a thousand years.[8]

Methodius of Olympus (d. 311 CE)

Methodius was, according to Quasten, "a highly educated man and an excellent theologian."[9] He was also a new creation millennialist. In his *Discourse on the Resurrection*, which will be referred to below, he ably refutes Origen's spiritualistic concept of the resurrection body. But in his earlier work *The Banquet of the Ten Virgins*, Methodius seems to have come under the influence of Origen's antipathy towards the body.[10]

[8] *Apocalypse of Elijah* 5:36-39, quoted from *The Apocalypse of Elijah based on P. Chester Beatty 2018* (ed. and trans. A. Pietersma and S.T. Comstock, with W. Attridge; SBL Texts and Translations, 19; Pseudepigrapha Series 9; Chico, California: Scholars Press, 1981).

[9] Quasten, *Patrology*, II, p. 129.

[10] In an extract from *Banq. Virg.* below (9:5), one will discover that Methodius expected believers to take on angelic (i.e. bodiless) form and ascend into heaven after the millennium. Quasten, *Patrology*, II, 132-33,

Nonetheless, he expresses a clear and historically-rooted doctrine of the millennium as set in the new creation.

Here are some extracts and comments:

> [The customs God appointed in the celebration of the feast of tabernacles] foretell the resurrection and the putting up of our tabernacle that had fallen upon the earth, which at length, in the seventh thousand of years, resuming again immortal, we shall celebrate the great feast of true tabernacles in the new and indissoluble creation... [At that time,] the fruits of the earth having been gathered in, and men no longer begetting and begotten, God [will be] resting from the works of creation.[11] (9:1)

In its use of Exodus typology and in its full affirmation that the millennium is set in the new creation, this work of Methodius particularly evokes the Epistle of Barnabas. It is notable that he does not expect there to be marrying and procreation in the millennium. Nor does he appear to expect the unrepentant to survive into the millennial period:

> By [Christ's] blood souls made safe and sealed [cf. Rev. 7:1-8] shall be preserved from wrath in the burning of the world; whilst the first-born, the sons of Satan, shall be destroyed with an utter destruction... (9:1)

The scenario Methodius proposes for the end of the millennium recalls that of Tertullian, in that it pictures an assumption into heaven for believers (or at least virgins). But one suspects the possible influence of Origen behind the implication here that even the resurrection body will somehow become obsolete:

> [On] the first day of the resurrection, which is the day of judgment, [I will] celebrate with Christ the millennium

points to some evidences that the earlier Methodius held a very high opinion of Origen. It is hard to decide, however, what proportion of the influence behind the eschatology of the *Banquet* belongs to Origen, and what belongs (directly or indirectly) to the earlier *Ascension of Isaiah* and to the tradition of some saints' ascension into heaven after the millennium as preserved by Irenaeus (*Adv. Haer*. 5:36:1).

[11] *Banq. Virg*. 9:1, trans. W. Clark, *The Writings of Methodius &c.* (ANCL, 14; Edinburgh: T. & T. Clark, 1906). See *ibid., De Creatis* 9.

> of rest, which is called the seventh day, even the true Sabbath. Then again from thence...as a follower of Jesus, "who hath entered into the heavens," [I myself shall] come into the heavens, not continuing to remain in tabernacles—that is, my body not remaining as it was before, but, after the space of a thousand years, changed from a human and corruptible form into angelic size and beauty, where at last we virgins, when the festival of the resurrection is consummated, shall pass from the wonderful place of the tabernacle to greater and better things, ascending into the very house of God above the heavens... (9:5)

As mentioned above, Methodius seems later to have rethought the matter and to have rejected this kind of spiritualized eschatology, realizing that it denigrated the body. He thus penned his *On the Resurrection* specifically in order to refute Origen's doctrine of spiritual resurrection.[12] In it he argues that since God created human beings in bodily form, to suppose that he would change them into angelic form (that is, make them bodiless) would be to suggest that the original design was faulty. As Methodius puts it,

> Neither did God, as if He had made man badly, or committed a mistake in the formation of him, determine afterwards to make an angel, repenting of his work...[13]

Methodius also applies the same argument to the physical universe. Whereas Origen claimed that the physical world would be destroyed and not re-created, Methodius affirms that the world will be re-created. Since the saints will be resurrected, so will the universe itself, so that "we who are renewed may dwell in a renewed world without a taste of sorrow..."[14]

Victorinus, Bishop of Pettau (d. c. 304 CE)

Victorinus wrote the earliest extant commentary on the whole Book of Revelation during the reign of the Emperor Gallienus

[12] See Quasten, *Patrology*, II, 136.
[13] *On the Resurrection* 11, in W. Clark, trans., *The Writings of Methodius.*
[14] *On the Resurrection* 9.

(258–260 CE). He is in fact the first to point out the recapitulative literary structure of Revelation:

> And the *trumpet* is the word of power. And it may be being repeated by the *bowls*, not as though it was [simply] said twice, but because what will happen only once is decreed by God that it will be, therefore it is said twice. Accordingly, whatever was said in the trumpets less [fully], it was said in the bowls more [fully]. Neither (should you be) regarding the order of sayings, because the sevenfold Holy Spirit, where He hurries through to the final times and the end, returns back to the same time and adds to what little He said. Nor (should you be) seeking order in the Apocalypse, for that is also false prophecy; rather be seeking the meaning.[15]

His comments on Revelation 21–22 make it clear that he sees the descent of the New Jerusalem (presumably accompanied by the creation of a new heavens and a new earth) as occurring at the Parousia, which he understands to be *the beginning* of the thousand years of Rev. 20:1-10:

> [Commenting on chapter 20:] At this same *first resurrection* will also appear the City and the splendid things expressed through this Scripture.
>
> [Commenting on chapter 21:] Therefore in the kingdom and in the first resurrection appears *the holy city*, of which he speaks, *descending from heaven, foursquare*, walled around with stones of different and precious and colored and various kinds, *like fine gold*, that is, bright. *In crystal*, he says, *are its street paved*; *the river of life flowing through the middle, and springs of waters of life; the tree of life around it, making different fruits for every*

[15] These quotations are from the edition of Martine Dulaey, *Victorin de Poetovio. Sur l'Apocalypse et autres écrits* (Source Chrétiennes 423. Paris: Les Éditions du Cerf, 1997), translated into English by Kevin Edgcomb, "St Victorinus of Poetovio: Commentary on the Apocalypse," accessed on the web 7/21/2019 at http://www.bombaxo.com/blog/?page_id=2181. My interpolations are in square brackets. Edgcomb indicates Victorinus's quotations of scripture with italics.

> *month; no light of the sun is there, because of a greater glory. The Lamb*, he says, *is its light.*
>
> [2]*Its gates*, truly, *are each a single pearl, three from each part, not closed*, but to be *open*. Scripture shows many reasons for the gifts of the kings of regions and nations, (kings) who will be servants, being brought there [Rev. 21:24]: he speaks of the subjection of the last ones, which we have treated.[16] But the city is not thus understood, as one (?) we have known; for we are not able to testify any further, without a guide, to that which we have heard and seen. ...
>
> [5]In this kingdom... all of creation will be saved and, by the command of God, will give forth the good things hidden in it... In this kingdom, *they will drink wine and be anointed with ointments* [Isa. 25:6-7] and they will be given to rejoicing [Isa. 25:9].[17]

Because Victorinus does not catch John's indications that Gog and Magog are the resurrected unrepentant, he understandably sees them as kings of the nations that are spared at the Parousia to serve the saints during the thousand years (see his comment on Rev. 21:24 above). He also expects these kings or their descendants to rebel at the end of the thousand years (Rev. 20:7-10),[18] which leads to an apparent contradiction: how can ordinary human beings have survived the radical dissolution and re-creation of the cosmos? Victorinus does not comment on this issue—in fact, he does not comment directly on Rev. 21:1 at all, possibly because he didn't know what to make of the conundrum implicit in his interpretation. The fact remains, however,

[16] I believe he is here referring to the generation that rebels at the end of the thousand years (Rev. 20:7-10). See his comments on Rev. 19:11-21 in nt. 18 below.

[17] *Ibid., in loc.*

[18] He comments on Revelation 19: "And a white horse, and one sitting upon him shows our Lord coming with the heavenly army to reign, at Whose coming all the nations will be gathered, and will fall by the sword. And others who were nobles will serve in the service of the saints; and of these (nobles) also he shows they will be killed in the end time, at the finish of the reign of the saints, before the judgment, after the release of the devil" (*ibid., in loc.*).

that Victorinus held two views which, when combined, amount to new creation millennialism: (1) the millennium starts at the Parousia of God and Christ, and (2) the new creation and the coming to earth of the New Jerusalem takes place at the Parousia of God and Christ.

The Modern Period

John Gill

Gill, an English Baptist minister and Calvinist theologian, is perhaps the most famous (English-speaking) biblical expositor of the 18th century.[19] He takes a full-fledged new creation millennialism approach in his Revelation commentary. He believes in a millennium that begins at the Parousia of God and Christ, he identifies the attack of Gog and Magog (Rev. 20:7-10) as the resurrection of the unrepentant, and he interprets John's vision of the new creation and the New Jerusalem's coming to the earth as a vision of the Parousia. Gill says in his comments on Rev. 20:8,

> Some think that [by Gog and Magog] the wicked living in the distant parts of the world, in the corners of the earth, are meant, who, upon Christ's coming, will flee thither, and remain in continual dread and terror to the end of the thousand years, when Satan will gather them together, and spirit them up against the saints; but this cannot be, because they will all be destroyed at the universal conflagration of the world [2 Pet. 3:7, 10-12]; nor will there be any in the new earth but righteous persons [2 Pet. 3:13]: but these will be all the wicked dead, the rest of the dead, who lived not again until the thousand years are ended, when will be the second resurrection, the resurrection of all the wicked that have been from the beginning of the world; and these, with the posse of devils under Satan, will make up the Gog and Magog army:

[19] Gill (1697–1771) published expositions of every book of the (Protestant) Bible from Genesis to Revelation. The paragraphs below are from his "Exposition of the Revelation of St. John the Divine," in *An Exposition of the New Testament*, III (1748).

> all the characters agree with them; these may be called nations, or Gentiles, being aliens from the true Israel of God, the dogs that will be without the holy city; these may be said to be in "the four quarters" of the world, since where they die and are buried, there they will rise and stand upon their feet, an exceeding great army; and as they will die enemies to Christ and his people, they will rise such…[20]

Gill says in his comments on Rev. 21:1-2,

> This vision…is to be understood of the glorious state of the church during the thousand years of Satan's binding, and the saints' living and reigning with Christ; the holy city, and new Jerusalem, is the same with the beloved city in Rev. 20:9. What is there briefly hinted, is here largely described and insisted on; this will be the time and state when the church of the firstborn, whose names are written in heaven [Heb. 12:23], will first meet together, and be brought to Christ, and be presented by him to himself a glorious church, without spot or wrinkle, or any such thing [Eph. 5:27], and Christ will reign gloriously among them: the seat of this church state will be the "new heaven" and "new earth" which John saw, and which are the same that Peter speaks of (2 Pet. 3:13), in which dwelleth righteousness, or in which righteous persons only dwell, for as the first heaven and earth both here and there are to be understood literally, so in like manner the new heaven and new earth; which will be new, not with respect to the substance, but their qualities…[21]

Sylvester Bliss

Bliss propounds a clear version of new creation millennialism, affirming, along with John Gill, that the millennium has the new

[20] Accessed 7/31/2017 at http://www.biblestudytools.com/commentaries/gills-exposition-of-the-bible/revelation-20-8.html.
[21] Accessed 7/31/2017 at http://www.biblestudytools.com/commentaries/gills-exposition-of-the-bible/revelation-21-1.html.

creation as its setting and that Rev. 20:7-10 narrates the resurrection and judgment of the unrepentant.[22]

Wolfgang Metzger

Metzger writes in Germany shortly after the end of WWII, and propounds new creation millennialism after having watched in horror as Hitler proclaimed his regime to bc "das tausendjährige Reich," that is, "the thousand-year reign".[23] Reading the text with new eyes, he realizes that in no sense is the "thousand-year reign" of Revelation 20 "this-worldly." It belongs entirely to the age to come and the new creation.

> By portraying the interregnum of Rev. 20:4ff. in an intentionally terse manner, John holds back the description of the nature and content of God's kingdom there at first, until he has seen it through to its last conflict (21:1ff.). Thus for John, the point of transition to the new age cannot (as ordinary chiliasm assumes) lie between Rev. 20:10 and 11.[24]

> Jesus will triumph, and in his triumph the old earth will flee, in order to make room for the new earth of the millennium. This is unquestionably the earth of the new age."[25]

Like Gill, Metzger rightly deduces that the hordes of Rev. 20:8-9 cannot be nations spared at the Parousia, in view of the radical break between the present age/creation and the millennium. They must instead be the "rest of the dead," the resurrected

[22] Bliss, Sylvester, *A Brief Commentary on the Apocalypse* (2nd edn; Boston: J. V. Himes, 1853), *in loc.* Accessed 7/31/2017 at http://www.gutenberg.org/ebooks/26639.

[23] See his "Das Zwischenreich," in *Auf dem Grunde der Apostel und Propheten* (Festschrift Bischof T. Wurm; ed. E. Loeser; Stuttgart: Quell-Verlag der Evangelische Gesellschaft, 1948), 100-18. See also the in-depth discussion of this article in Mealy, *After the Thousand Years* (see p. 10 nt. 1 above), 47-57.

[24] "Das Zwischenreich," 105.

[25] "Das Zwischenreich," 107.

unrepentant released from the abyss together with the devil "after the thousand years are completed" (cf. 20:3, 5, 7).[26]

Eckhard Schnabel

New Testament scholar Eckhard Schnabel, persuaded by the evidence presented in my monograph *After the Thousand Years*, follows my interpretation closely in his popular book *40 Questions on the End Times*.[27]

Summary

I am aware of nine[28] others besides myself who have published works interpreting Revelation's millennium as starting with the Parousia of God and Christ and having its setting in the new creation. Papias of Hierapolis, Melito of Sardis, the writer of the Apocalypse of Elijah, Methodius, and Victorinus of Pettau all lived and wrote within two centuries of the writing of Revelation, establishing the most ancient pedigree possible for this view. John Gill, Sylvester Bliss, Wolfgang Metzger, and Eckhard Schnabel clearly articulate versions of new creation millennialism in the modern period, each of them concluding (as I independently concluded) that Gog and Magog are to be understood as the resurrected unrepentant. There are doubtless many other readers and scholars of the New Testament who share these insights, but my researches have simply failed to discover them.

[26] "Das Zwischenreich," 113-15.

[27] Grand Rapids, MI: Kregel, 2011.

[28] I have left the (pseudonymous) Epistle of Barnabas off of this list because his view is probably independent of the Book of Revelation. He is a new creation millennialist thanks to his day-age eschatological schema, not because he read about the thousand years in Revelation and interpreted it there. It could, however, be retorted that a Christian new creation millennialist eschatological model nearly contemporary with Revelation but independent of it is of equal or even greater evidential value than would have been the case if Pseudo-Barnabas had simply derived his view from reading Revelation. If anything, it suggests the possibility that the idea of a future thousand-year age set in the new creation *was already in circulation among Christians before Revelation was written*.

Index of References

OLD TESTAMENT

Genesis
1:1-2:4 151, 152
1:26-28 62
1:26-27 59
2 137
3:1-15 25
3:1-5 137
5:1-3 59
19:24-25 46
19:27-28 46
22:17 31
32:12 31

Exodus
15:7 114
16 78
16:33 78
24:10 145
25-30 54
25:18-22 16
32:32-33 79
40:34-38 54

Leviticus
23:9-14 114
26:11-12 55

Deuteronomy
26:1-11 114
29:23 46, 47
33:2 21

Judges
7:12 31

1 Samuel
4:4 16
13:5 31

2 Samuel
6:2 16
7:14 58

1 Kings
4:20 31
5-8 54
6:20 81

2 Kings
1:10-14 31
19:15 16

1 Chronicles
13:6 16

2 Chronicles
3:8 81
6:18 54
7:1-3 54

Job
38:4-11 52

Psalms
2 22
2:1-3 23
2:1 23
2:1 LXX 16
2:5 23
2:7-9 23
2:8-12 123
2:8-9 78
2:9 21
2:11 23
24:1 62

36:9 58
45 14, 18, 83
45:1-7 123
51:15 37
68:17 21
69:28 79
80:1 16
89:9-11 52
90:4 28, 30
96:13 19
99:1 16
110:1-6 123
145:8-9 137

Proverbs
26:11 38

Ecclesiastes
1:7 53

Isaiah
1:13 152
2:10 65
2:19 65, 70
2:21 65, 70
4:5-6 81
5:1-7 148
5:24 114
9:6-7 123
10:22 31
11:4 21
11:6-12 123
11:9 52
24-27 26, 33, 34, 36, 45, 50, 111, 135, 136
24 25
24:1-22 26
24:1-20 34
24:3-6 26
24:5-6 141
24:5 51
24:8 142
24:10-11 33
24:14-16 142, 143
24:16 143
24:18-20 26, 51, 143, 144
24:19-27:5 166
24:21-27:5 62, 123
24:21-23 25, 26, 33, 135
24:21-22 34, 136, 144
24:22 26, 34
24:23-27:3 35
24:23-26:8 34
24:23-25:12 56
24:23 26, 36, 144
25:1-2 145
25:4 81
25:6-7 160
25:7-8 56, 145, 146
25:7 57
25:8 34, 54
25:9 160
26:10-11 34, 35, 42, 43
26:10 33, 146
26:11 31, 34, 146
26:12-19 34
26:13-19 110, 111
26:13 111, 147
26:14-19 83
26:14 111, 112, 115, 147
26:17-19 51
26:18 111
26:19 111, 112, 115, 147
26:20-27:5 35
26:20-21 36, 147
26:21-27:5 43
26:21 71
27:1-5 137
27:1 25, 34, 148
27:2-5 36, 148
27:2-3 35
27:4-5 35
27:4 114
27:5 35
33:11 114
34 47, 136
34:5 48
34:6 48
34:9-10 48
34:10-11 48
35:10 55
37:6 16
40:10-11 17
40:10 26
42:9 58
43:18 55
43:19 58
47:14 114
48:6 58
49:2 21

51:17 115
52:1 115
54:4 73
54:5 18
55:1 58, 59
57:15-21 36, 37, 137
59:20 17
60:1 42, 115
60:2 42
60:19 42
62:4-5 18
62:11 26
63:1-6 20
63:1-3 20
65-66 73, 136
65 72, 73
65:17-25 47
65:17-22 118
65:17-20 72, 73
65:17-19 55
65:17 71-73, 91
65:18 73
65:19 55
65:20 73
66:15-16 70
66:22 47, 71, 72, 91

Jeremiah
2:12-13 59
2:13 58
3:14-17 42
5:22 53
17:12-13 42
23:5-6 123
23:6 80
33:15-16 80
33:22 31
49:18 46, 47
50:39-40 46, 47

Ezekiel
1:4-28 16
1:22 145
1:24 17
10:1-22 16
10:1 16, 145
27-39 135
32:26 32
34:24 22
34:28 22
36-38 50
36:25-27 22
37:21 22
37:23 22
37:24 22
37:25 22
37:27 54, 56
38 45
38:1-13 32
38:4 32
38:8 32
38:11-12 32
38:19-23 32
39 22
39:17-29 166
39:17-20 22
39:26 22
39:27 22
39:29 22
43:2 17
47:1-12 53
47:8-9 136

Daniel
2:47 21
3:1-6 13
7 12, 27, 40, 44, 94, 99, 128, 135
7:7-8 94
7:7 27
7:8-14 123
7:8 27, 99
7:9-15 94
7:9-11 41
7:9-10 27, 40
7:9 19
7:10-14 83
7:11-14 12, 13, 102
7:11 27, 99
7:13-14 27, 89, 128
7:13 94
7:14 129
7:17-18 123
7:18 27, 29, 62, 83, 89, 102, 128, 129, 133
7:20-27 99
7:20-25 94
7:21-22 12, 27
7:21 10, 27, 102
7:22-27 123
7:22 94
7:25-27 12, 27, 102

7:25 10, 24
7:26-28 128
7:26-27 83, 89, 94
10:6 19
12:1 32, 79
12:3 129
12:7 12, 24
12:11-12 12

Hosea
6:5 21

Joel
2:3-5 114
2:32 17
Obadiah
1:17-21 17
1:18 114

Micah
5:2-5 123

Nahum
1:10 114

Habakkuk
2:3-4 124
2:14 52

Zephaniah
2:9 46, 47

Zechariah
2:10-11 56
2:11 54
3:8-9 78
14:7 73
14:9 73
14:12-19 73
14:12 73
14:17 73, 74

Malachi
4:1 114

NEW TESTAMENT

Matthew
2:1-31 99
3:11-12 114
3:12 18
3:17 23
5:10 125
5:26 136
5:29-30 136
6:9 60
9:15 18
10:37-38 32
10:38 61
11:23 26
11:27 121
12:29 96
12:41-42 136
12:45 96
13:30 18, 114
13:39 18
16:27 21, 120
17:5 23
19:18-30 125
19:28 77, 89, 120
20:8 96
20:10 96
21:8-9 17
21:28 96
21:36 96
22:1-14 18, 19
22:5 96
22:23 108
24:22 28, 75
24:29-31 66
24:30-31 117
24:31 28
24:42-44 24
24:43-44 71
25:1-10 18
25:31-46 136
25:31 89, 120
25:31 21
25:41 62, 136
26:17 96
27:64 96
28:18-20 121-23

Mark
1:11 23
2:19-20 18
3:27 96
8:38 21, 120
9:7 23
9:42-48 136

11:8-10 17
12:18 108
12:20 96
13:1-27 99
13:20 28, 75
13:24-27 66
13:26-27 117
13:27 28
14:12 96
16:9 121

Luke
3:16-17 114
3:22 23
5:35 18
6:20-26 133
8:31 26
9:26 21, 120
9:35 23
10:15 26
10:22 121
11:2 125
11:21-22 96
11:26 96
11:31-32 136
12:35-40 24
12:39-40 71
12:59 136
14:12-14 112, 113, 115
14:18 96
16:5 96
16:8 127
16:23 26
16:31 108
19:11-12 125
19:16 96
19:36-38 17
20:27 108
20:29 96
20:34-36 69
20:35-36 133
20:35 30, 32, 107, 110, 112, 113, 115, 133, 134
20:36 61, 73
20:38 108

John
1:1-18 21
1:1 121
1:12-13 60
1:14 121
1:20 96
1:30 96
1:49 23
3:29 18
3:35 121
5:25-29 29, 32
5:25 133
5:28-29 32, 133
6:32-58 78
6:48-50 28
7:37-38 59
7:37 58
12:1 109
12:9 109
12:12-16 17
12:17 109
12:24-26 61
13:3 121
15:1-5 43
15:18-19 126
17:2 121

Acts
1:1 96
1:6-8 123
2:27 26
2:31 26
3:19-21 124
4:25-27 23
5:3 96
13:33 23
13:46 33
17:1-9 116
17:28 60
20:18 96
24:15 113
26:23 96

Romans
5:3-5 123
6:4-5 116
6:5 123
6:8 112, 123
6:13 116
7:6 116
8:3 121
8:17-23 112
8:17 123
8:18-23 51, 77, 90
8:18-21 124, 125
8:18 138
8:20-21 90
8:23 90
8:34 121
8:35-36 123
9:5 121
10:7 26, 108
11:26-27 17
12:5 43

16:27 129

1 Corinthians
2:7 130
2:9 73
4:4 124
5:5 96
8:6 121
10:11 130
10:17 43
10:26 62
12:12-27 43
13:12 52
14:30 96
15 119
15:1-9 118
15:12 113
15:20-24 113
15:22-28 119, 120
15:22-25 133
15:22-24 133
15:22-23 112
15:22 114
15:23 120
15:26 120
15:28 120
15:46 95
15:47 95
15:52 28, 112

2 Corinthians
4:3-4 126
4:3 96
4:4 96
4:17-18 138
5:17 116
8:9 121
11:2 18, 87
11:14 96

Galatians
1:3-4 126
1:4 124
4:26 18, 81

Ephesians
1:20-22 121
1:21 130
1:22-23 43
2:1-2 127
2:2 124
2:5-6 116
2:7 130
2:14-22 43
4:10 121
4:15-16 43
4:22-24 116
4:25 43
5:14 111, 115, 116
5:23-32 87
5:27 162
5:30-32 18
6:10-12 96
6:11-12 127
6:12 124

Philippians
1:5 96
1:29 123
2:7-8 121
2:9-11 121
3:10-11 112, 114, 133
3:20-21 112, 113
3:20 81

Colossians
1:15-18 121
1:18 43
1:24 43
1:26-27 73
2:12-13 116
2:19 43
3:1-3 116
3:1 121
3:4 113
4:16 18

1 Thessalonians
1:9 120
2:18 96
4-5 119
4:13-5:3 66
4:13-17 116-19, 133
4:13 118
4:15-17 28, 113
4:15 118
4:16-17 118
5:2 71
5:4 71

2 Thessalonians
1:5-2:12 99
1:5 33
1:7-10 70, 71
1:7-8 21
1:11 33
2:12 120
1 Timothy
2:13 96
5:12 96
6:15 21

2 Timothy
2:6 96
2:8-12 123
2:10-13 113
2:26 96
4:16 96

Titus
3:5 89

Hebrews
1:1-2 130
1:2 23, 121
1:3-10 121
1:5 23
2:9-18 121
2:9-15 138
3:3-4 121
4:7-8 121
5:1-10 138
5:5 23
8-9 95
9:4 78
9:26 130
10:12-13 121
10:27 34
10:35-39 124
11:12 31
12:1-11 123
12:2 121
12:22 81
12:23 162
13:8 131
13:15 37

James
4:4 127
4:13-5:11 133

1 Peter
1:5-7 123
1:20 131
4:11 131
4:13 123
5:8 96

2 Peter
2:22 38
3:3-13 155
3:3-9 91
3:5-13 70, 71
3:7 161
3:8 151
3:10-12 161
3:11-13 90, 91
3:13 155, 161, 162

1 John
2:15-17 124, 127
3:13 127
4:4 96
5:19-20 124
5:19 96, 127

Jude
1:14 21
1:25 131

Revelation
1:1-2 19
1:1 64
1:5 19
1:7 94, 99
1:8 16, 74, 80
1:9-22:17 38, 76
1:11 96, 149, 154
1:13 29, 94, 99
1:15 19
1:16 21
1:17 96
1:18 26, 29, 31
2-3 77, 149
2:4 96
2:5 96
2:7 17, 28, 77
2:8 96
2:10-11 29
2:10 28, 78, 96
2:11 37, 41
2:12 21
2:13 96
2:16 21
2:17 28, 78
2:18 19
2:21 121
2:25-28 14, 28
2:25-26 21
2:26-28 78
2:26-27 22, 26
2:26 78
2:27 21, 78
2:28 28, 79
3:1 154
3:3 24, 71
3:4-5 17, 21, 28
3:4 32, 79
3:5 79
3:7 19
3:11-12 28, 87
3:12 80
3:14-22 133

3:14 19, 149
3:18 79
3:21 26, 28, 39, 62, 79, 138
4-22 85
4-5 85
4:1-6 51
4:1-2 139
4:1 96, 145
4:2 42
4:3-5:14 139
4:5-8 80
4:6-8 16
4:6 57, 145
4:8 16, 74, 80
5:1-14 42
5:1-10 138
5:1 26
5:9-10 68
5:10 62, 79, 87
5:11 21
5:13 39
6 85
6:1-11 139
6:1-3 80
6:1-2 19
6:1 19
6:3-4 19
6:5-6 19
6:7-8 19
6:8 26
6:9-11 19, 40, 93
6:12-17 19, 40, 65, 66, 74, 88, 99, 134, 139
6:13-14 31
6:14-16 38
6:14 19, 39, 51, 76, 143, 145
6:15-17 14
6:15-16 65
6:15 22
6:16-17 20, 26, 39
6:16 39
7:1-8 139
7:9-17 17, 40, 55, 66, 139
7:9-12 87
7:9-10 39
7:9 79
7:13-17 138
7:13-15 79
7:13-14 17
7:14 66
7:15-17 26, 87, 88
7:15 55, 81
7:17 17, 121
8-9 85
8:1-9:21 139
8:5 16
8:6-9:19 75
8:7 141
9:1 26
9:2 26
9:3 32
9:8-21 142
9:18-21 141
10:1-7 139
10:5-7 16
10:8-11 139
11 85
11:2-3 12, 24
11:3-8 11
11:5-18 26
11:7 26, 32, 97, 99
11:15-19 14, 16, 40, 87, 88, 99, 139
11:15-18 79, 80
11:15-17 102
11:15 16, 20
11:17-18 16, 74, 75
11:17 16, 26
11:18-19 26
11:18 16, 22, 23, 28, 30, 40, 43, 51, 68, 75, 102
11:19 16, 19, 51, 78, 80, 81
12-13 85, 104
12 10, 100, 104
12:1-13:18 139
12:1-13:1 135
12:1-17 103, 132
12:1-5 42
12:1 13
12:4 10
12:5 21, 22
12:6 12, 24, 99, 103
12:7-13:1 104
12:7-11 100

12:7-9 10, 26
12:7-8 103
12:7 100
12:8-13:1 97
12:9-18 96
12:9-11 98
12:9 101
12:10-12 40
12:10-11 102
12:10 10, 20, 26, 102, 103
12:11 79, 102
12:12-17 103
12:12 12, 24, 80, 102, 103
12:13-17 14, 99
12:14 12, 24, 103
12:17-13:17 100
12:17-13:4 101
12:17-13:1 100
12:17 12, 27, 31, 99, 102
13 11, 66, 94, 97, 98
13:1-8 99
13:1-7 27
13:1 12, 32, 42
13:2 12
13:3-17 11
13:3-4 98
13:3 42
13:5-7 99
13:5 12, 24, 103
13:6 80, 81
13:7-8 67, 98
13:7 27, 97, 98, 102
13:8 12, 33
13:9-10 98
13:11 32
13:12 12
13:14-17 13, 98
13:14 42
13:15-17 67
13:15 97, 102
13:16-17 12
13:16 22
13:18 13
13:19 22
13:8 98
14 12
14:1-5 17, 87, 139
14:1 17
14:2 17
14:4 18
14:6-13 12
14:6-8 140
14:9-12 140
14:9-11 46, 48
14:9-10 20, 67
14:13 40, 140
14:14-20 40, 140
14:14-16 18
14:14 94
14:15 81
14:17 81
15-16 85
15 12
15:1-4 66
15:1 140
15:2-4 140
15:2 51, 57, 145
15:5-16:17 140
15:5-8 80
15:5 81
16 12
16:1 12
16:3 75
16:8-9 26, 142
16:10 13
16:12-16 13, 101
16:12-14 13
16:13-17 104
16:13-16 23
16:13-14 24
16:14-16 26
16:14 16, 26
16:15 71
16:17-21 40, 88
16:17-20 38, 39, 75, 76
16:17 57, 80
16:18-21 140
16:18 143, 144
16:20-21 143, 144
16:20 31
17-18 85
17 13, 94
17:1-19:4 11
17:1-18:24 140
17:1-8 42
17:1 11
17:3 13, 27, 99
17:4 13
17:5 11

17:6 11, 13
17:8-14 99
17:8 12, 13, 26, 27, 32, 33, 97
17:9-11 27
17:11-14 23, 24
17:11 12, 13
17:12-17 13
17:12-14 13, 14
17:14 16, 21
17:15 11
17:16-18 13, 42
17:16 143
17:18 11, 13
18 13
18:1-19:4 13
18:2 145
18:3 11, 13
18:8 27, 48
18:9-10 11
18:10 13
18:14-19 13
18:16-19 42
18:18 13
18:21 42, 145
18:22 142
18:23 11, 13
18:24 10, 13
19-21 63, 82
19-20 166
19 83, 85, 94
19:1-21 140
19:1-2 142, 143
19:3 47, 48, 145
19:4 13, 14
19:5-21:8 9, 11, 14, 63, 132, 134
19:5-20:15 49
19:5-21 15
19:5-10 14
19:5-9 40, 54
19:5 11, 13, 15, 16, 54
19:6-9 26, 84, 86
19:6-7 17
19:7-8 18, 53, 79
19:7 53
19:8-9 29
19:8 21, 29, 53
19:9-10 18
19:9 28
19:11-21:4 64
19:11-20:10 9
19:11-20:3 53
19:11-21 14, 15, 18, 40, 43, 63, 67, 68, 82, 93, 94, 160
19:11-15 78
19:11-12 19
19:11 16, 145
19:13-15 20
19:13 21
19:14-20:10 166
19:14-20:5 120
19:14-15 78
19:14 21, 26, 62, 66, 68, 79, 83
19:15-16 26
19:15 20, 22
19:16 21
19:17-20:9 56
19:17-20:2 46
19:17-21 16, 54, 99, 101, 104, 134, 135
19:17-18 21
19:17 68
19:18 22
19:19-20:10 34
19:19-20:6 102
19:19-20:3 144
19:19-21 22
19:19-21 13, 19, 23, 26
19:19-20 24
19:19 26
19:20 27, 38, 41, 46
19:21-20:10 38
19:21 15, 21, 26, 31, 68, 75
20 10, 26, 46, 84, 85, 93, 100, 105, 106, 131-33, 163
20:1-15 15
20:1-10 9, 25, 34, 37-39, 46, 49, 62,

	67, 86, 91-93, 96, 105, 106, 133, 134, 159
20:1-6	105, 150, 165
20:1-3	12, 15, 24, 26, 45, 63, 69, 83, 84, 96, 98, 100, 102, 104, 132, 135, 140
20:1-2	100, 103
20:1	26, 100, 103
20:2	34, 94, 101, 137, 148
20:3	25, 26, 30-32, 94, 96, 98, 101-103, 160
20:4-10	44, 45
20:4-6	15, 26, 34, 40, 43, 53, 54, 63, 79, 83, 84, 92, 94, 106, 107, 110, 132, 140, 160
20:4-5	27, 45, 65
20:4	27-30, 33, 40, 44, 62, 83, 93-95, 97, 99, 102, 133, 135, 145, 147
20:5-10	44
20:5	28-31, 41, 83, 94, 95, 147, 160
20:6	26, 28-30, 37, 41, 61, 62, 93-95, 133, 145, 157
20:7-15	120
20:7-10	15, 25, 26, 31, 43, 45, 49, 50, 53, 54, 61, 63-65, 76, 83, 84, 97, 99, 103, 104, 120, 137, 140, 151, 160-62, 166
20:7-8	46, 69, 137, 146
20:7	97, 100, 160
20:8-9	32, 33, 41, 42, 45, 47, 50, 163
20:8	50, 65, 96, 98, 161
20:9-10	147, 148
20:9	32, 34, 38, 41, 42, 44, 46, 69, 87, 98, 99, 145, 146, 160
20:10	9, 15, 34, 41, 45, 46, 48, 146, 148, 163
20:11-15	33, 38, 43-45, 53, 54, 64, 65, 76, 83, 84, 95
20:11-12	42, 140
20:11	38-40, 43, 51, 76, 77, 88, 163
20:12-15	44, 45
20:12-13	45
20:12	39-41, 44, 45, 83
20:13-15	41-43, 50, 61, 65, 83,

84, 86, 140
20:13 26, 40, 41, 43-45, 136
20:14-15 38, 44, 46
20:14 120
20:15 15, 26, 41
21-22 159
21:1-22:5 14, 51, 85, 86, 140
21:1-8 42, 50, 51, 61, 62, 84, 86, 134, 160
21:1-7 14, 15, 61
21:1-4 64, 145, 146
21:1-3 136
21:1-2 15, 42, 54, 74, 77, 89, 145, 151, 162
21:1 51, 84, 95, 136
21:2 53, 81, 87, 157
21:3-7 88
21:3-6 87
21:3-4 54, 56
21:3 52, 54, 55, 60, 81
21:4 57, 73, 95
21:5-6 57
21:5 76
21:6-7 28, 58
21:6 57, 58
21:7 59
21:8 14, 38, 60
21:9-22:5 42, 81, 157
21:9-27 145
21:9-11 42
21:9 81
21:10-11 52, 81
21:11 42
21:18 81
21:21 145
21:22-23 26
21:22 81
21:23 42, 144, 145
21:24 160
21:27 42
22:1-5 28, 78, 138
22:1-3 37
22:1-2 53, 136
22:3-4 26
22:4-5 131
22:4 52
22:5 15, 27, 29, 42, 52, 62, 99, 140, 144, 145
22:6-11 140
22:8-9 19
22:9 42
22:12-17 140
22:12 17, 26, 28
22:13 96
22:14 28
22:16 28, 78, 79
22:17 17, 28, 87
22:18-21 140

JEWISH SOURCES

1 Enoch
1.9 21
8.6-9 42
24.1-25.5 42

4 Ezra
7.26-43 116
8.52-54 116

Apoc. Baruch
29-30 116
29.3-8 150

Apoc. Elijah
3.36-39 156

Life of Adam and Eve
29.7-10 116
48.1-3 116
51.1-2 116

Midrash
Genesis Rabbah
96 116

Philo
Vit. Mos. 2.65 89

Josephus
Ant. 11.66 89

CHRISTIAN AUTHORS

Augustine
City of God
20.7 150

Epistle of Barnabas
6.13 153
6.18-19 28, 153
15.4-5 152, 153
15.7 152
15.8 152

Eusebius
Hist. Eccl.
3.39.11-12 150
5.33.3 150
5.36.1 157
7.25.6-17 149

Irenaeus
Against Heresies
5.33.4 149

Jerome
Comm. in Exod.
36 153

Melito of Sardis
Discourse before Antoninus Caesar
Frag. 154, 155

Methodius
Banq. Virg.
9.1 157
9.5 156-58

De Creatis
9 157

De Res.
9 158
11 158

Origen
de Principiis
2.2-3 150

Victorinus
Comm. in Apoc.
19.11-21 160
20.1-20 160
20.1-10 159
20.7-10 160
21.9-22.5 157, 160
21.24 160

CLASSICAL

Arratus, Phaenomena
5 60

Arrian, Tactics
28.2 115

Diodorus Siculus, Library
13.109 114

Made in the USA
Middletown, DE
12 September 2021

48162066R00099